P9-ANZ-004

THE SAXON SAVIOR

THE SAXON SAVIOR

The Germanic Transformation of the Gospel in the Ninth-Century Heliand

G. RONALD MURPHY, S.J.

New York Oxford
OXFORD UNIVERSITY PRESS
1989

Oxford University Press

Oxford New York Toronto
Delhi Bombay Calcutta Madras Karachi
Petaling Jaya Singapore Hong Kong Tokyo
Nairobi Dar es Salaam Cape Town
Melbourne Auckland

and associated companies in
Berlin Ibadan

Copyright © 1989 by G. Ronald Murphy, S.S.J.

Published by Oxford University Press, Inc.,
200 Madison Avenue, New York, NY 10016

Oxford is a registered trademark of Oxford University Press

All rights reserved. No part of this publication may be reproduced, stored in a retrieval system, or transmitted, in any form or by any means, electronic, mechanical, photocopying, recording or otherwise, without the prior permission of Oxford University Press.

Library of Congress Cataloging-in-Publication Data
Murphy, G. Ronald, 1938–
The Saxon savior: the Germanic transformation of the Gospel in the ninth-century Heliand / by G. Ronald Murphy. p. cm.
Bibliography: p. ISBN 0-19-506042-3
1. Heliand. I. Title
PF4000.M8 1989 839′.1–dc20 89-3419 CIP

9 8 7 6 5 4 3 2 1

Printed in the United States of America
on acid-free paper

To

Tom Gavigan, S.J.,

Knight Exemplar,

and

the Soldiers

of

Inigo's Company

PREFACE

At the early beginnings of northern Germanic literature there stands a unique masterpiece of religious epic poetry—the ninth-century *Heliand* 'Savior.' In its almost 6,000 lines of alliterative verse, its unknown author completed an almost impossible task. He transformed the text of the entire Gospel by a poetic reimaging of its content in Saxon terms. His generous-souled reinterpretation was able to find a place for many of the old northern religious concepts and images in his Gospel. Its conception was, I believe, motivated by deep pastoral sympathy for the Saxon people, so recently and violently converted to Christianity.

Readers familiar with the *Crist* and the *Dream of the Rood* will find a kindred spirit in the *Heliand*—but one that stands on its own soil and is neither derivative nor directly dependent on the religious poetry of Anglo-Saxon England. The *Heliand* author set himself a different task, one calling for both great fidelity to a given text and great freedom of mind in reimaging it. The author was, as we shall see, no mere translator (as were several of his contemporaries) nor was he a propagandist full of zeal and ideas but lacking in human feeling for his text and for his Saxons. The resulting effect of the *Heliand* on the conversion of the peoples of northern Germany and the Scandinavian countries may have been considerable if we can judge by the expression of Christian art in Germanic forms beginning at this period from Jutland to the Isle of Man.

Above all, the *Heliand* is the meeting place of the Christian Gospel and Germanic culture. More than a hundred years after its probable time of origin, it was still being copied in full. One of the extant manuscripts, *C*, dates from the second half of the tenth century. In its pages Christianity and northern European warrior culture came far closer to a synthesis than in the earlier *Beowulf* or in the *Chanson de Roland*. This synthesis provided an evangelical basis for the imaging of Christian discipleship in soldierly terms and opened the imagination and the conscience to create the ideal of the northern Christian soldier—the knight. This evangelical synthesis, it might be further argued, even though originally intended as poetic metaphor, facilitated, and was the embodiment of a founding element of the culture of Europe.

Why is this epic so little read in our day? This is a question I find difficult to answer. The Old Saxon in which it is written is indeed part of the problem, but something not intrinsic to the poem may be more of a factor: the book has had a somewhat turbulent history of use and misuse in modern times. The *Heliand* was not published until 1830—a thousand years after it was written, and in a greatly changed cultural world.

Its first successfully popular interpreter was a theologian who read the epic as the "germanized" Gospel since it removed the Gospel message from its non-German context and placed it in a context he thought far more appropriate to its content. This nationalistic interpretation remains a lingering block for many readers and complicates reading the *Heliand* and its "germanization" of the Gospel in its original intercultural Saxon context. (More of this in the first chapter.) During the Nazi era this same unfortunate nationalistic view of the *Heliand* reemerged and the epic suffered "aryanizing" misuse and false praise. To this day one must use the word germanization with great sensitivity and precision when referring to the *Heliand*.

Scholars have also used the *Heliand* for many purposes somewhat remote at times from regarding it as an epic Gospel poem. It has been seen as an archaeological site from which fragments of pre-Christian Germanic culture could be sifted. Philologists have studied it carefully for early Germanic legal vocabulary and to reconstruct North-Sea Germanic. Paleographers returned to the manuscripts to study letters and erasures to determine the number of scribes who produced the versions we now have. More recently, structural studies have been made of the *Heliand*, with mixed success. The *Heliand* is rich from many scholarly points of view, but it is a human treasure and a literary masterpiece when read as what it is: a poetic transformation of the Gospel for the Saxons.

My purpose is to explore what I consider to be the poetic heart of the text and to read it in the context of the religious climate of the times. I hope to uncover some of the art of the beautifully deft mind that could imagine and create a culturally transformed Gospel via poetic analogy. The *Heliand* author possessed a deeply respectful attitude toward the values of Germanic religion and culture, but an equally careful regard for his Christianity. Thus, his "germanization" is not crude, paganizing theology, but a moving blend of spiritual sensitivity and Germanic poetry. The *Heliand* is not primarily the work of a sociopolitically oriented artist—though elements of the socio-political world are important to it—and it may in its "Saxonizing" actually be antipangermanic. The author seems to me to be a subtle defender of the defeated Saxons rather than a propagandist for the Christian conquerors.

Lastly the *Heliand* may have seemed too daunting because of the very scholarship surrounding it. A pity. The *Heliand* contains a wealth of spiritual and intercultural contemplation, which should be most appealing and instructive in our day of a shrinking earth, where culture must, of necessity, bump against culture and religion against religion.

In a place and time that insisted on religious conformity or death, the unknown author of the *Heliand* managed the impossible and did it with grace. He remained faithful to the orthodox Christian teaching of the Gospel, and yet in his contemplation of that Gospel imagined an almost unthinkably new and different form of Christianity, thereby transforming the Gospel into the traditional religious imagery and values of his people. It is well worth reading and understanding today for it is neither propaganda nor a sermon, but rather most profoundly a work of contemplative compassion and intercultural communication. I hope that what I have written will encourage the *Heliand* to be appreciated and read again, both by students of literature and by scriptural and pastoral theologians. In order to examine the exact nature of the *Heliand* as a poetic transformation of the Gospel, I have found it most useful to compare the literal Old High German translation of Tatian's *Diatessaron* with the Old Saxon of the *Heliand*.

In the present volume I have also included English translations or paraphrases (my own attempts unless otherwise noted) with the Old Saxon, Old High German, German, and Latin texts. These will be for the amusement of those who do not need them and, I hope, a help for those who do. For the reader who would like a contemporary version of the *Heliand*, there is the excellent German translation of Felix Genzmer and the archaic-style English version of Marianna Scott. I hope to have a new version finished in the near future.

Washington, D.C. G. R. M.
March 1989

ACKNOWLEDGMENTS

It is customary in this part of a book to thank as many of those whom you can remember who have contributed to your work. At the end of the list the editor is almost always mentioned. I would like to reverse the order and first thank Cynthia Read for her great gift of sensitivity to the *Heliand* and for her enthusiasm for these pages. She and her assistant, Inger Forland, and Paul Schlotthauer showed the determination and flexibility that made it possible for this project to "come to the light of men," and made its completion a smooth and happy path for its author.

I would further like to thank the staff and benefactors of the Research and Study Center at Centreville, Maryland. for providing me with a pleasant and inviting atmosphere for research and writing. In particular I am grateful for the support of Sis Geuting, Patsy Bremmer, and the Raskob Foundation for both inspiration and financial help.

With regard to the manuscript itself, I am deeply indebted to those anonymous readers who carefully read the text, and who, with painstaking accuracy, took the time to indicate corrections and improvements. I hope your reward will be in seeing many of your suggestions contributing to a much improved manuscript. I am very greatly in your debt.

To my colleagues of the Georgetown faculty I would like to say a word of appreciation, but to none more than to Heidi Byrnes, who gave up hours of her time to go through the manuscript line by line, seeking lost umlauts and incomplete thoughts and leading them all safely home.

Still tied to the pencil and the typewriter as I am, the reader will appreciate with what heroic courage and patience my assistants managed to get this book into a contemporary final form. Cynthia McMullen singlehandedly translated my handwriting and three other foreign languages into the necessary machinery and disks, a task that would have daunted even Beowulf. Eric Byrnes added his expertise with the computer's word hoard and, with the help of Richard O'Brien, S.J., produced the final version.

To all acknowledged and unacknowledged, known and unknown, who have in any way helped, I am deeply grateful. It would be a lack of *courtoisie*, though, to fail to mention among the unknown, one before whom I stand in awe: the poet-monk, who over a thousand years ago produced the magnificent *Heliand*, and modestly did not give his name.

CONTENTS

THE SAXON SAVIOR

1
A GERMAN CHRIST?

In 1845 and again in 1862 A.F.C. Vilmar published his enthusiastic interpretation of the *Heliand*: *Deutsche Altertümer im Heliand als Einkleidung der evangelischen Geschichte* 'German Antiquities in the Heliand as Clothing for the Gospel Story.'[1] In it he argues forcefully that the *Heliand* is *das Christentum im deutschen gewände* [*sic*—Vilmar's orthography] 'Christianity in German robes'[2] and that the image of Jesus Christ has been so transformed that it is *ein deutscher Christus* 'a German Christ'.[3] This controversial fundamental thesis has been largely rejected by the scholarship of the present day, and yet I think there is indeed much to be said for it. Vilmar's conservative, nationalistic tone and his almost insulting acceptance and use of the clichés of German cultural superiority have justifiably had a great deal to do with this rejection. His basic concept of the *Heliand* as a German Gospel, however, deserves serious reexamination and refinement.

In order to be fair to the *Heliand* itself, it certainly should be viewed as a part of the evangelical tradition of dual-cultural expression. One observes the coexistence and interaction of Semitic and gentile expressions of the Gospels themselves, especially in those of Luke and John. The *Heliand* is also a part of the specific historical context of the expansion northward of Byzantine and Roman Christianity for the conversion of Slavic and Germanic peoples. Most important, however, the *Heliand* should be seen in the local Germanic context of this northern thrust. Vilmar errs badly, I believe, when he projects nineteenth-century, pan-Germanic ideals onto what is clearly a local ninth-century *Saxon* religious epic which, moreover, contains dark tones of dissatisfaction with the "pan-Germanic" Frankish power in Aachen. The words "Saxon" and "Frank" were certainly understood in the ninth century. What would Vilmar's "German" Christ have meant, if anything, to the author of the *Heliand*?

In order not to throw out the baby with the bath water, however, I think the *Heliand* can be accurately interpreted both as a *saxonization* and as a *northernization* of the Gospel. It might more properly be described in English as "The Saxon Christ" or "The North Sea Gospel."

Let us proceed to a critical reexamination of Vilmar's work and method. In his Introduction he states his purpose clearly enough: he wishes to research "wie das evangelium von dem volke aufgenommen worden ist, wie die sendboten ihre lehre den deutschen hörern nahe gelegt, und wie die volksstämme versucht haben, sich dem evangelium und das evangelium ihrer anschauung gerecht zu machen"[4] [how the Gospel was accepted by the people, how the missionaries made their teaching clear to their German listeners, and how the tribes attempted to adapt themselves to the Gospel and the Gospel to their point of view]. Since he insists on using a univocal concept of "German," Vilmar systematically excludes any appreciation of the profound ambiguities in the poem, specifically of two of the deepest undercurrents in the *Heliand*: the figure of *Peter* as the central model of a loyal knight, and the sympathy of the poem for the situation of the Saxons as a conquered people. He states categorically on the same page: "In unserem gedichte ist weder von römischer hierarchie noch von den Frankenschwertern eine Spur zu finden." [In our poem there is not a trace to be found of either Roman hierarchy nor of Frankish swords].

This is an era when popes consistently referred to themselves as the vicars of Peter and were seen in iconography to be on the throne of Peter. Of course there is no Vatican hierarchy in the *Heliand*, but "Peter" is everywhere and, as we will see, is described both in the scene of the walking on the water and in the swordplay at the arrest of Jesus as being especially close to Christ. The Frankish swords are indeed nowhere to be seen, but resentment against their wielders can be found both in the description of Herod and his men and in the crucifixion. This Vilmar was unwilling even to consider when he interpreted both of these scenes, owing, it seems, to his theological and Germanic presuppositions.

Vilmar made his observations under eight categories:

1. Epic Form (*epische Form*)
2. Mythology (*Mythologie*)
3. View of Nature (*Naturanschauung*)
4. Attitude of Mind (*Gesinnung*)
5. Morals, Household, Possessions, Financial Worth (*Sitte, Hausleben, Besitz, Vermögen*)
6. Relations [Family] (*Verwandtschaft*)
7. People and King (*Volk und König*)
8. The Life of a Warrior (*Kriegerleben*)

In them he hoped to show that the *Heliand* poet had produced the Gospel in "German" form. In each category he assembled truly admirable philological and literary observations. In Epic Form, he clearly shows that the *Heliand* is in the tradition of the older Anglo-Saxon biblical epics and delightfully explores possible allusions to Grendel and his mother when the devil tempting Christ is called *mirki* 'murky.'[5]

In Mythology, Vilmar accurately attends to the concepts of *wurd* 'Fate' and *metod* 'God-the-Measurer'[6] in their roles in the *Heliand*, but as his method is more philological than visualizing, he misses the descent of the Holy Spirit onto the shoulder of Christ in the scene of his Baptism at the River Jordan. The same method enables him to give prominence to the unusual impact of the word *wan* 'light breaking out of darkness,'[7] but he fails to notice that the two scenes of 'light breaking out of darkness' occur at the beginning and end of the poem, at the birth and at the resurrection, and nicely bracket the 'light breaking through' in the transfiguration scene at the center of the whole composition. This highlighting technique gives an *inclusio* structure to the whole epic.

In Attitude of Mind, after some unfortunate preaching on the Germans as a *Naturvolk*, which again misdirects him, and annoys the contemporary reader, Vilmar comes to the crucial question of the *Heliand*'s purpose. He sees it in the frequent repetition of injunctions against doubting: that we *hugi ni latan tuiflien* 'do not let our minds doubt'.[8] Interestingly Vilmar again reveals his method: a good philological approach combined with an interpretive assumption of nineteenth-century German cultural superiority. He observes that the root of the word to doubt, *tuiflian*, rests on the idea of two, as in "two-faced" and, as such, is evil and is specifically opposed to the unified, simple, straightforwardness of the "German." As he thus leaves philology and switches over to the cultural side of his interpretational method, all hope for seeing repeated *tuiflian* in the cultural context of ninth-century Saxon revolts and conversions disappears. Vilmar goes his own way, imagining a united, ideal, ninth-century Germany:

> Die edelsten, grossartigsten characterzüge der Nation, die was sie war, ganz war, die lauterkeit und festigkeit der gesinnung und die innere einheit und einigkeit mit sich selbst übertrug der Dichter als ein rechter apostel des evangeliums, auf die personen seiner heiligen geschichte.[9]
>
> *The noblest and most magnificent characteristics of the [German] Nation, a nation that was through-and-through what it was, cleanness and determinedness of mind, inner unity and unity with oneself, were transferred by the poet, as a good apostle of the Gospel, onto the persons in his holy story.*

Any attempt to see the *Heliand* as an effort to overcome the alienation of the Saxons and to reconcile them to the faith originally forced upon them is precluded by the exclusion of any effort to examine the real social situation of the day.

When Vilmar uses simply philological method, as in his description of Christ as a clan lord and the disciples as the warrior-knights of his retinue, *Gefolgschaft*, of the crucifixion as mixture of a crucifixion and a hanging, containing both the hammer and nails and a noose[10] and the burial as occurring in a Mediterranean tomb, but the resurrection as being from a loose earth grave by the sea, he makes a real and undeniable contribution to the poetic appreciation of the *Heliand*. At these points he attempts to visualize the scene and to delineate its internal structure. For a moment Vilmar abandons his dual method of philological analysis and cultural presumption, and succeeds.

Since the time of Vilmar's famous interpretation, scholars have debated the question of the "germanization" of the Gospel in the *Heliand* and, with the exception of some unremarkable and predictably enthusiastic scholarship during the Nazi era, have tended to an understandably nervous ambiguity about it.

One of the oblique attacks comes from Hulda Göhler who claims that the nature of Christ in the *Heliand* is to be traced primarily to early Christian dogma rather than to the Germanic world.[11] This certainly correct observation, however, seems to rest more on an examination of the orthodoxy of the theological sources of the *Heliand* (Bede, Rabanus, Gregory) than on a literary examination of the poem itself, but Göhler does manage successfully to refute the remark of Vilmar that, in the *Heliand*, the divinity of Christ recedes into the background.[12] However this method does not adequately approach the question of a poetic re-expression of the content of the whole Gospel story into Germanic form, which is, quite correctly, the question Vilmar set himself to answer.

Walter Baetke would not even concede, as Göhler did, that the *Heliand* can be interpreted as depicting Christ as the leader of a band of noble warriors, *Gefolgschaft*, and maintained that this interpretation of Vilmar's rested on a false interpretation of the appropriate texts.[13] He correctly insists that there is no worship of Fate or *wurd*[14] in the *Heliand*, but does not delineate or explore its carefully allotted place in the intercultural world of the *Heliand* Gospel.

Recent studies in the vocabulary of the *Heliand* have confirmed an abundance of terms from Germanic law and religion in the poem, but confusion exists as to the degree of force that they maintained. Weisweiler and Betz write: "Die auffälligsten Reste des Heidentums im Hel.–Wortschatz sind die durch den alten *Schicksalsglauben* geprägten Ausdrücke. Auch sie sind sozusagen getauft und haben dadurch eine christliche oder mindestens neutrale Färbung erhalten."[15] [The most striking remains of paganism in the vocabulary of the *Heliand* are the expressions formed by the old *belief in fate*. Even they have been "baptized" and have thereby received a Christian or at least a neutral coloration]. Weisweiler and Betz have identified a serious problem: the degree of coloration. This can be approached only by the study of vocabulary in its context and use within the work. In addition Weisweiler and Betz have adduced a large list of vocabulary taken from Germanic law including Christ's position in the Sermon on the Mount:

"Als Leiter der Volksversammlung, des germ. things, erscheint Christus in der vom Hel.-Dichter erfundenen Einleitung zur Bergpredigt"[16] [As the leader of the assembly of the people, the Germanic *thing*, is how Christ appears in the introduction to the Sermon on the Mount, an introduction that is the creation of the *Heliand* poet]. The authors conclude that the use of legal terms very closely follows the biblical story and is "in der viel diskutierten Linie einer 'Germanisierung des Christentums'"[17] [in the much discussed line of a "germanizing of Christianity"].

In order to ascertain more closely, if possible, the nature of the "Germanizing" of the *Heliand* and the possible intent of its author, let us proceed again to a close reading of the poetry of the *Heliand* in its original context as a poem of the Gospel for the fallen Saxons.

Notes

1. Vilmar claims in the second edition to have changed nothing from the first. I have been able to gain access only to the second (Marburg: N.G. Elwert'sche Universitäts-Buchhandlung, 1862), hereafter cited as Vilmar.
2. Vilmar, p. 1.
3. Ibid.
4. Ibid., p. 2.
5. Ibid., p. 8.
6. Ibid., pp. 11–17.
7. Ibid., p. 24.
8. Ibid., p. 32.
9. Ibid., p. 33.
10. Ibid., p. 50.
11. "Das Christusbild in Otfrids Evangelienbuch und im Heliand" in *Zeitschrift für deutsche Philologie* 59 (Stuttgart: Kohlhammer, 1935).
12. Ibid., p. 36.
13. Baetke, Walter. "Die Aufnahme des Christentums durch die Germanen" in *Vom Geist und Erbe Thules* (Göttingen: Vandenhoeck, 1944), p. 101.
14. Ibid., p. 98.
15. Joseph Weisweiler and Werner Betz, "Deutsche Frühzeit" in Friedrich Maurer and Heinz Rupp, *Deutsche Wortgeschichte*, 3. Aufl., Bd. 1 (Berlin: Walter de Gruyter, 1924), p. 84.
16. Ibid., p. 70.
17. Ibid.

2

JESUS IS *DROHTIN*

VIII. Si quis deinceps in gente Saxonorum inter eos latens non baptizatus se abscondere voluerit et ad baptismum venire contempserit paganusque permanere voluerit morte moriatur.

From now on, should anyone hidden among the Saxons as a non-baptized person wish to remain in concealment, who disdains to come to baptism and wishes to remain a pagan, let him be put to death. (Capitulatio de partibus Saxoniae 'Law Code for the Saxon Territories'[1] *797* A.D.*)*

In the thousand-year history of Christianity's missionary efforts in Europe, I doubt if there is any page as brutal as that of Charlemagne's thirty-three-year war of conversion and conquest of the Saxons of northern Germany. It is thus all the more remarkable that such a fascinating work as the *Heliand* should be written by an unknown Saxon at a time when the Saxons were still offering sporadic resistance to the imposition of the Carolingian empire and church.

The *Heliand* is an epic poem of the life of Christ, written in Old Saxon (with some Frankish and Frisian elements) in alliterative verse. It is the first epic work of German literature, a masterpiece antedating the extant *Nibelungenlied* by some four hundred years. It is a cousin of Anglo-Saxon biblical literature and its author seems to have been familiar with the poetic tradition of the British Isles in which Christianity expressed itself so felicitously in northern forms.

The author was most probably a monk of Fulda, Corvey, or Werden. Paleographic studies of the *M* manuscript of the *Heliand* by Bischoff have led him to connect its handwriting style with Corbie, the motherhouse of Corvey, and thus with an origin at Corvey. *M* may indeed have been copied at Corvey, but one need not conclude from this that the original *Heliand* was necessarily composed at the same monastery. No one maintains that *M* is the original itself, but rather a later, ninth-century, copy. Thus the question of place of origin remains open.[2] I favor Fulda both for the reason of its being an Anglo-Saxon foundation, which was given responsibility for the conversion of the Saxons, and, essentially, because of the presence there of Rabanus Maurus as abbot. Rabanus's broadminded tendencies with regard to non-Christian religious expression would speak well for his support of a monk attempting to write a saxonized version of the Gospel.[3] I am further biased in this opinion by the geographical situation of Fulda on the Fulda River, which is a tributary of the Weser and thus flows through the middle of Saxony into the North Sea. Riverbank and seashore scenes are a specialty of the author of the *Heliand.* This criterion, however, does not exclude Corvey or Werden, and is thus not a strong argument. Indeed it does not seem that scholars have found it possible to resolve the question of origin once and for all.

The poem was originally untitled and was not called the *Heliand* 'Savior' until 1830 when its first editor, Andreas Schmeller, published it as *Heliand. Poema Saxonicum seculi noni.* Flacius Illyricus, a Protestant apologist of the sixteenth century, wishing to justify the translation of Scripture into the vernacular, cites as supporting evidence from a now lost prose *Praefatio* 'Preface' that a certain man of the Saxon people, *cuidam viro de gente Saxonum*, had already been told to translate poetically the Old and New Testaments into the German language: *in Germanicam linguam poetice transferre.*[4] Though there are some difficulties with this so-called *Heliand* preface, still, if genuine, it tells us something interesting about the *Heliand*'s author: that he was an epic poet of standing among his people, *apud suos non ignobilis vates*, and that the work was commissioned by the Emperor *Ludovicus pijssimus Augustus*, presumably Louis the Pious, Charlemagne's son and troubled successor. Furthermore the lost preface gave the purpose of Louis in commissioning the work as "so that not just the literate but also the illiterate might have the sacred reading of the divine teachings opened up to them" [quatenus non solum literatis verum etiam illiteratis sacra divinorum praeceptorum lectio panderetur]. This preface thus not only helps reinforce the dating of the poem at c. 830 A.D. (Louis the Pious died in 840), but it also returns us to the issue of the "opening up" of the Gospel to the Saxons.

The conversion of the Saxons really goes back to St. Boniface in the century preceding the *Heliand*. Boniface was originally called by his Anglo-Saxon name of Wynfrid before Pope Gregory II changed it to Bonifacius. He was born in Wessex c. 675 and was educated in the Benedictine abbeys of Exeter and Nursling. After being ordained a priest he went to Frisia as a missionary at about the age of 40 in the year 716. He was not successful. In 719 Boniface secured a papal commission to convert the pagan Germans and, significantly, was instructed to use the Roman baptismal formula rather than the Celtic form of the ritual, which he and others must have been using from the monasteries of the British Isles. We know that when he returned to German territory he was much more ruthless both toward the German pagans and toward the Irish missionary clergy there, whom he regarded as too paganized. Can it be that he objected to the earlier missionaries' attempts to "accommodate" ritual and formulation to the native Germanic culture and insisted instead on romanization of the pagans in the preaching of the Gospel?

The famous incident of felling the sacred oak of Thor at Geismar while a great crowd of pagans stood silently cursing Boniface as the enemy of their gods, and concealing their shock and hatred in their hearts: *inimicum deorum suorum intra se diligentissime devotabant*, is probably the paradigmatic incident of non-accommodation. The whole incident is described in Willibald's *Life of Boniface* as follows:

> Roborem quendam mirae magnitudinis qui prisco paganorum vocabulo appelatur robor Idsis, in loco qui dicitur Gaesmere, servis Dei secum adstantibus succidere temptavit. Cumque mentis constantia confortatus arborem succidisset, magna quippe aderat copia paganorum, qui inimicum deorum suorum intra se diligentissime devotabant.[5]

> *He attempted to cut down a tree of tremendous size which in the old time vernacular of the pagans is called the tree Idsis, located in a place called Gaesmere, with the servants of God all standing close to him. As he, strengthened by his unswerving determination, cut the tree down, there was a great number of pagans present who kept on cursing this enemy of their gods under their breath with the greatest fervor.*[5]

Boniface converted by confrontation and direct threat of violence (he was backed up by Charles Martel's Frankish soldiers at the tree), and his method appeared to be so successful that there seems at the time to have been little need to worry about German hearts and minds. He even had the sacred oak subsequently sawn into planks and with them built a church dedicated to St. Peter, the patron saint of his apostolic protector.

Visiting Rome again in 737, Boniface was urged by the pope to attempt the conversion of the old, or continental, Saxons. Perhaps in partial fulfillment of this charge, he founded the celebrated monastery of Fulda in 744. St. Boniface died a martyr's death at the hands of the Frisians in 754, but left a tradition of non-accommodating missionary methods based on a powerful and even ruthless personality.

Charlemagne's birth date is not absolutely certain, but it is thought that he may have been born only about fifteen years after the death of St. Boniface. He was the next to attempt to overcome the paganism of the Frisians and the Saxons. He admired the revered Boniface very much and it is perhaps no surprise that he who also had the uncompromising personality of the martyr, would tend to employ similar missionary methods—and to carry them to an incredible extreme.

His similarity to Boniface in thinking that the direct method was the only one is shown in his destruction of the Irminsul. This pillar, or perhaps tree trunk, was located at a shrine near the headwaters of the River Lippe. It was probably a representation of Yggdrasil, the cosmic tree, the tree of life, support of the universe, and the center of Saxon worship.

In view of the tree of life and the tree of the knowledge of good and evil in the Garden of Eden story, it is interesting to speculate how this tree shrine might have been "baptized" by an accommodating missionary. It was, however, connected with the worship of Thor and Woden, and Charlemagne predictably saw only one way to handle the situation. In 772, a generation later, he followed Boniface's precedent, marched with his army into Saxony, advanced quickly to the Irminsul, and utterly destroyed it.

The less military weapon by which the *Heliand* author wished to see the tree of paganism chopped down, however, is the song of the Gospel. After praising the four evangelists in his introductory chapter, he adds that they were inspired by the Holy Spirit:

> that sea scoldin ahebbean helagaro stemnun godspell that guoda ...
> *they should lift up [begin to tell] the good Word of God with their holy voices ...*
>
> efto derƀi thing, firinwerk fellie (I, 24–25 and 27–28)[6]
> *so that it might chop down every perverse thing, every work of evil.*

The unusual image of "felling" evil is one that no doubt was not lost on Saxon listeners. The allusion manages both to concede that it may be necessary that certain evil things be chopped down, but to imply as well that the four evangelists' Gospel has sufficient power itself, if spoken and understood, to accomplish the defeat of evil—without the help of Frankish axes.

Charlemagne had decided for the romanization of the faithful instead of the germanization of the faith, and even insisted for a time that, in the Romance-speaking parts of his empire west of the Rhine, the Mass be celebrated in a pure form of Latin that the vernacular speakers of the contemporary *lingua romana rustica* 'country Latin' could no longer comprehend. He seems to have harbored a special resentment for his Saxon cousins to the northeast who had preserved and were clinging to ancient Germanic tribal values that Charlemagne himself may have guardedly admired despite his rejection of them.

The Saxons had preserved a form of individualistic democracy that had once been described with unabashed respect by Tacitus. Saxony was divided into the four provinces of Westfalen, Engern, Ostfalen, and Nordalbingien which were probably more territorial than political entities. Political power was in the local clan territory (the *Gau*) and in the leading local families or nobles. There were no cities among the Saxons, but rather local fortified communities surrounded by wooden palisades (*falen*), built on a height. Such a hill-fort community was called a *burg*. Thus the *Heliand* author is conjuring up a locally familiar image of the city of the Caesars when he constantly refers to Rome as *Rumuburg*. Translators generally render this into English as Romeborough or Romeburg. I think more of the original imagery could be retained if we translated instead: Fort Rome, Fort Jerusalem, and even Fort Nazareth, thus preserving the image of a stockade.

The lack of a central city might be thought of as a weakness in regard to the need for organization in time of war, but just the opposite seems to have been the case. The lack of a single strong point to be overcome, a main head to be cut off, made the Saxons extremely resilient in their prolonged warfare with the centralist government and culture of Charlemagne's empire. The very need of Charlemagne to invade and search, and destroy repeatedly, not only significantly large areas, but almost the entire land area of Saxony in order to force submission, shows just how successful the prolonged guerrilla style of warfare really was with its dispersed seats of Saxon government.

This should not be taken to mean that the Saxons were not capable of overall organization. The Saxons also had retained the *Volksversammlung* or annual general assembly of the people. Charlemagne also had kept this custom and we know it from him as the March (later, May) Field. At the general assembly the Saxons could elect an overall leader or commander-in-chief, if there was to be a war. He could be chosen by lot from the nobles who were at the heads of the clan territories or he could be selected at the annual assembly. His authority, however, lasted only for the duration of the war.[7] This arrangement seems to bear some resemblance to the system of the North American Indians who also had a separate chief for wartime whose power ceased at the end of hostilities; power then reverted to the peacetime chief. This system would not have been amusing in Aachen, but it provided the Saxons both with long-term decentralization in peace and temporary centralization in war. It also avoided the danger of having an overarching military figure who could demand unwavering and lifelong loyalty. The permanent loyalty of a Saxon, be he noble, freeman, or boundman, was to his local personal lord or *drohtin*. It is in this remarkable sense that *drohtin* is used in the *Heliand* for Jesus.[8]

The tragic warfare that constituted the conditioning circumstance under which the Saxons received the Christian faith is described both by Einhard in sections 7 and 8 of his *Vita Caroli Magni* (with unaccustomed bursts of intemperate language concerning the Saxons) and by the authors of the *Annales Regni Francorum*.

Einhard gives his version in section 7 of his *Vita*:

> Post cuius finem Saxonicum, quod quasi intermissum videbatur, repetitum est. Quo nullum neque prolixius neque atrocius Francorumque populo laboriosius susceptum est; quia Saxones, sicut omnes fere Germaniam incolentes nationes, et natura feroces et cultui daemonum dediti nostraeque religioni contrarii neque divina neque humana iura vel polluere vel transgredi inhonestum arbitrabantur. Suberant et causae, quae cotidie pacem conturbare poterant, termini videlicet nostri et illorum poene ubique in plano contigui, praeter pauca loca, in quibus vel silvae maiores vel montium iuga interiecta utrorumque agros certo limite disterminant, in quibus caedes et rapinae et incendia vicissim fieri non cessabant. Quibus adeo Franci sunt irritati, ut non iam vicissitudinem reddere, sed apertum contra eos bellum suscipere dignum iudicarent. Susceptum est igitur adversus eos bellum quod magna utrimque animositate, tamen maiore Saxonum quam Francorum damno, per continuos triginta tres

annos gerebatur. Poterat siquidem citius finiri, si Saxonum hoc perfidia pateretur. Difficile dictu est, quoties superati ac supplices regi se dediderunt, imperata facturos polliciti sunt, obsides qui imperabantur absque dilatione dederunt, legatos qui mittebantur susceperunt.[9]

At the conclusion of this struggle [with the Lombards] the Saxon war that seems to have been only laid aside for a time was taken up again [this was in 772, hostilities had been going on for some time, presumably]. No war ever undertaken by the Frank nation was carried on with such persistence and bitterness, or cost so much labor, because the Saxons, like almost all the tribes of Germany, were a fierce people, given to the worship of devils, and hostile to our religion, and did not consider it dishonorable to transgress and violate all law, human and divine. Then there were peculiar circumstances that tended to cause a breach of peace every day. Except in a few places, where large forests or mountain ridges intervene and made the bounds certain, the line between ourselves and the Saxons passed almost in its whole extent through an open country, so that there was no end to the murders, thefts, and arsons on both sides. In this way the Franks became so embittered that they at last resolved to make reprisals no longer, but to come to open war with the Saxons. Accordingly war was begun against them, and was waged for thirty-three successive years with great fury... It could doubtless have been brought to an end sooner, had it not been for the faithlessness of the Saxons. It is hard to say how often they were conquered, and, humbly submitting to the king, promised to do what was enjoined upon them, gave without hesitation the required hostages, and received the officers [legates] sent them from the king.[10]

What Einhard records here as simply a neutral historical fact—that Charlemagne sent Frankish officers to Saxony to attempt to keep the Saxons in subjection—avoids describing what the Saxon reaction to these officers must have been, presumably the same as the reaction of any occupied people to the representatives of the occupying power. Is it not the same as the reaction of the Jews in the New Testament to their puppet rulers also sent by a Roman emperor? The author of the *Heliand* is expressing the deepest sympathy with his Saxon brethren when he suggests this brilliant and, I think, very thinly veiled allusion to the situation in Saxony as he describes King Herod in the introductory song:

> Than habda thuo drohtin god
> Romanoliudeon farliwan rikeo mesta,
> habda heriscipie herta gisterkid,
> that sia habdon bithwungana thiedo gihuilica
> habdun fan Rumuburg riki giwunnan
> helmgitrosteon, saton iro heritogon
> an lando gihuem, habdun liudeo giwald,
> allon elitheodon. Erodes was
> an Hierusalem oƀer that Iudeono folc
> gicoran te kuninge, so ina *thie keser* tharod
> fon Rumuburg riki thiodan
> satta undar that gisiđi. *Hie nie was thoh mid sibbeon bilang*
> *aƀaron Israheles eđiligiburdi,*
> *cuman fon iro cnuosle, neuan that hie thuru thes kesures thanc*
> *fan Rumuburg riki habda,*
> that im warun so gihoriga hildiscalcos
> abaron Israheles elleanruoƀa
> *suiđo unwanda wini, than lang hie giwald ehta.*
> [italics added] (I, 53-70)

At that time the Lord God had granted to the Roman people the greatest kingdom, had strengthened the hearts of their army so that they had subdued many a nation. They had, from Fort Rome, won an empire, those comrades under helmet; their military governors ruled in every land, had power over the people, in every foreign nation. Herod was chosen to be king in Jerusalem over the Jewish people, since he was sent there by the Emperor, the

> *powerful ruler, from Fort Rome to those warrior companions, even though he was not related to them by clan, nor did he come from the kin from those noble-born sons of Israel. It was only by Caesar's grace from Fort Rome that he held power, that warriors came to owe him allegiance, descendants of Israel, famous for their strength, his very faithful friends—as long as he held power.* [italics added]

By highlighting and elaborating what in New Testament theology is only a footnote, and by making the nature of Herod's rule and Jewish collaboration a sly main point of his Introduction, our poet has not only managed to transpose the geographical situation of Palestine into that of Saxony, but also the geopolitical situation as well. In so doing he evokes Saxon empathy with the sons of Israel, "noble-born" and "famous for their strength," subject to a foreign ruler at the whim of Caesar Augustus (Charlemagne's full title, after 800, was: *Carolus Augustus a Deo Coronatus* 'Charles Augustus [Caesar Augustus] Crowned by God'), and begins setting the stage for the Saxon warrior's eventual identification with Peter and the disciples.

The *Heliand* poet's ingratiating method may seem innovatively propagandistic, but it may be in reality a return to the earlier pre-Bonifacian Irish missionaries' attempts at conversion. The severity of the thirty-three years of warfare and the inner resentment of the losers may also have necessitated a return to the earlier methods in order to facilitate a real internal conversion. Then, too, the carefully drawn visual parallels between Saxony and Israel smack more of resentment turned to meditative contemplation than of goal-oriented propaganda. The ceaseless resistance in Saxony during the eighth and ninth centuries is chronicled in the *Royal Frankish Annals*:

> Tunc nuntius veniens, qui dixit Saxones rebellatos et omnes obsides suos dulgtos et sacramenta rupta et Eresburgum castrum per mala ingenia et iniqua placita Francos exinde suadentes exiendo; ... attamen quantum illi plus pavore perterriti fuerunt, tanto magis christiani confortati omnipotentem Deum laudaverunt, qui dignatus est suam manifestare potentiam super servos suos. Et inde

fugam arripientes Saxones, persecuti sunt eos Franci interficientes illos usque ad flumen Lippiam... Et ibi placitum publicum tenens et consilio facto cum Dei adiutorio sub celeritate et nimia festinatione Saxonum caesas seu firmitates subito introivit. Et Saxones perterriti omnes ad locum, ubi Lippia consurgit, venientes ex omni parte et reddiderunt patriam per wadium omnes manibus eorum et spoponderunt se esse christianos et sub dicione domni Caroli regis et Francorum subdiderunt. Et tunc domnum Carolus rex una cum Francis reaedificavit Eresburgum castrum denuo et alium castrum super Lippiam, ibique venientes Saxones una cum uxoribus et infantibus innumerabilis multitudo baptizati sunt et obsides, quantos iamdictus domnus rex eis quaesivit, dederunt. Et perfecta supradicta castella et disposita per Francos scaras resedents et ipsa custodientes reversus est domnus Carolus rex in Franciam.[11]

776 A.D. ... *a messenger came with the news that the Saxons had rebelled, deserted all their hostages, broken their oaths and by tricks and false treaties prevailed on the Franks to give up the castle of Eresburg... the more the Saxons were stricken by fear, the more the Christians were comforted and praised the almighty God who deigned to reveal his power over his servants. When the Saxons took flight, the Franks followed on their heels as far as the River Lippe, slaughtering them ... He [Charlemagne] held his general assembly and, after deliberation, suddenly broke through the fortifications of the Saxons with God's help. In great terror all the Saxons came to the source of the River Lippe; converging there from every point they surrendered their land to the Franks, put up security, promised to become Christians, and submitted to the rule of the Lord King Charles and the Franks. The Lord King Charles with the Franks rebuilt the castle of Eresburg and another castle on the River Lippe. The Saxons came there with their wives and children, a countless number, and were baptized and gave as many hostages as the Lord King demanded. When the above castles had been completed and Frankish garrisons installed to guard them, the Lord King Charles returned to Francia. (pp. 54–55)*[12]

It seems quite clear from the juxtaposition of baptism and giving hostages that good King Charles was nothing if not a realist and that our annalist is a loyal clerk of the Bonifacian school of missionary activity.

multitudo Saxonum baptizati sunt et secundum morem illorum omnem ingenuitatem et alodem manibus dulgtum fecerunt, si amplius inmutassent secundum malam consuetudinem eorum, nisi conservarent in omnibus christianitatem vel fidelitatem supradicti domni Caroli regis.[13]

777 A.D. . . . *Many Saxons were baptized and, according to their custom, pledged to the king their whole freedom and property if they should change their minds again in that detestable manner of theirs and not keep the Christian faith and their fealty to the Lord King Charles.*

Et cum audissent Saxones, quod domnus Carolus rex et Franci tam longe fuissent partibus Hispaniae per suasionem supradicti Widochindi vel sociorum eius secundum consuetudinem malam iterum rebellati sunt . . . sed illi rebelles ad Renum et multas malicias facientes, ecclesias Dei incendentes in sanctemonialibus, et quod fastidium generat enumerandi. (p. 52)[14]

778 A.D. . . . *(This is the time of the loss of Roland at Roncevalles.) When the Saxons heard that the Lord King Charles and the Franks were so far away in Spain, they followed their detestable custom and again revolted, spurred on by Widukind and his companions . . . these rebels advanced as far as the Rhine at Deutz [opposite Cologne], plundered along the river, and committed many atrocities such as burning the churches of God in the monasteries and other acts too loathsome to enumerate. (p. 56)*

One of these loathsome acts may have been cannibalism. Not all among the Saxons seem to have been of Vilmar's Germanic virtue, and the Christian Franks were genuinely shocked at Saxon cannibalism as the imposition of the death penalty in the *Capitulatio de partibus Saxoniae* demonstrates:

> Si quis a diabolo deceptus crediderit secundum morem paganorum virum aliquem vel feminam strigam esse et homines comedere et propter hoc ipsam incenderit vel carnem ejus ad comedendum dederit vel ipsam comederit, capitis sententiae punietur.[15]
>
> *If anyone, being deceived by the devil, should believe as the pagans do, that some man or woman is a witch who eats people and for this reason should have him or her burned or should give his or her flesh to be eaten, or should eat the witch, he shall suffer the loss of his head.*

The *Lex Salica* had also acknowledged the problem but seems to have treated it a bit more prosaically:

> Si stria hominem commederit ... dinarios VIIIM qui faciunt solidos CC culpabilis indicetur.
>
> *If a witch [male or female] should eat a human being, he shall be judged guilty of 8,000 dinarii or 200 solidi.*

> Et cum reversus fuisset, statim iterum Saxones solito more rebellati sunt, suadente Widochindo ... Sumptisque armis non quasi ad hostem in acie stantem, sed quasi ad fugientum terga insequenda spoliaque diripienda, prout quemque velocitas equi sui tubrat, qua Saxones pro castris in acie stabant, unusquisque eorum summa festinatione contendit. Quo cum esset male perventum, male etiam pugnatum est; nam commisso proelio circumventi a Saxonibus, paene omnes interfecti sunt... Hoc audiens domnus Carolus rex una cum Francis quos sub celeritate coniungere potuit, illuc perrexit et pervenit usque ad locum, ubi Alara confluit in Wisora. Tunc omnes Saxones iterum convenientes subdiderunt se sub potestate supradicti domni regis et reddiderunt omnes malefactores illos, qui ipsud rebellium maxime terminaverunt ad occidendum IIII D; quod ita et factum est. (Waitz, pp. 60, 63, 62)[16]

782 A.D. *... As soon as he (Charles) returned (to Francia), the Saxons, persuaded by Widukind, promptly rebelled as usual... They (the Franks) took up arms and going after booty instead of facing an enemy lined up for battle, everybody dashed as fast as his horse would carry him for the place outside the Saxon camp where the Saxons were standing in battle array. The battle was as bad as the approach. As soon as the fighting began, they were surrounded by the Saxons and slain almost to a man... When he heard this the Lord King Charles rushed to the place with all the Franks that he could gather on short notice and advanced to where the Aller flows into the Weser. Then all the Saxons came together again, submitted to the authority of the Lord King and surrendered the evildoers who were chiefly responsible for this revolt to be put to death—four thousand of them. This sentence was carried out. (pp. 59–61)*

Et tunc rebellati sunt iterum Saxones solito more et cum eis pars aliqua Frisonum. (p. 66)[17]

784 A.D. *... The Saxons rebelled as usual and some Frisians along with them. (p. 61)*

Ten years later we find the annalist continuing to report the same events:

Inde motus est exercitus partibus Saxoniae per duas turmas... Saxones congregantes se in campo, qui dicitur Sinistfelt, praeparantes se quasi ad pugnam; cum vero audissent se ex duabus partibus esse circumdatos, dissipavit Deus consilia eorum, et quamvis fraudulenter et christianos se et fideles domno regi fore promiserunt. (pp. 94-96)[18]

794 A.D. *... From Frankfurt the army set out in two detachments for Saxony... The Saxons gathered in the plain called Sindfeld and prepared for battle. But when they heard that they were surrounded on both sides, God frustrated their intentions and they promised, with no such*

> *thing in mind [emphasis added], to become Christians and loyal to the king. (p. 73)*

Every year thereafter the same dreary sequence repeated itself with the Saxons occasionally able to revolt for a short time, but surrendering promptly and promising to become Christians at the sight of Charlemagne's army in Saxon territory, even despite the eventual capitulation of Widukind. In 804 Charlemagne performed a massive deportation of Saxons into Frankish territory as an attempt at a "final solution":

> 804 A.D. ... Imperator Aquisgrani hiemavit. Aestate autem in Saxoniam ducto exercitu omnes, qui trans Albiam et in Wihmuodi habitabant, Saxones cum mulieribus et infantibus transtulit in Franciam et pagos Transalbianos Abodritis dedit. (Wirtz, p. 118)[19]

> *The emperor spent the winter at Aachen. But when the summer came he led an army into Saxony and deported all the Saxons living beyond the Elbe and in Wihmuodi with their women and children into Francia and gave the districts beyond the Elbe to the Obodrites.*

Nonetheless, Nithard mentions a Saxon revolt in 840, almost in passing, as though it still were expected as an annual event and not as important as the wars between Louis the Pious's sons:

> Eodem tempore Lodhuwicus partem exercitus inibi causa custodiae reliquerat, et Saxonibus sollicitatis, obviam illis perrexerat. Quamobrem Lodharius parvo conflictu custodes fugere compulit, Renum cum universo exercitu transiens, Franconofurth iter direxit.[20]

> *At that time Louis had left part of his army as a garrison in Worms and had gone to meet the Saxons who were in revolt. But after a small skirmish Lothair put the defendants to flight and, crossing the Rhine with his entire army, headed for Frankfurt.*[21]

Despite the massive deportation of Saxons by Charlemagne as a last-ditch effort to destroy their resistance to the empire and

Christianity, in 842 there were still enough of them (the *Stellinga*) willing and able to revolt against Charlemagne's grandson. Since this uprising was ten years later than the probable date for the composition of the Heliand, it gives us all the more insight into the compelling circumstances of its composition. Nithard has the following entries:

> October 842... Lodhuwicus etenim in Saxonia seditiosos, qui se, uti prefatum est, Stellinga nominaverant, nobiliter, legali tamen caede compescuit...
> November 842... Stellinga in Saxonia contra dominos suos iterum rebellarunt; sed praelio commisso nimia cede prostrati sunt. (Pertz, as above, pp. 50 and 53.)[22]
>
> *Louis, however, distinguished himself by putting down, not without rightful bloodshed, the rebels who, as I said before, called themselves Stellinga...*
> *... the Stellinga [exact meaning uncertain] in Saxony rebelled against their lords. But when it came to battle they were put down in a great bloodbath.*[23]

The *Heliand* author had a task ahead of him. Thus Heinz Rupp's conclusion that the purpose of the *Heliand* was to combat superstition and to bring Christianity closer to the "illiterate," and that the author fulfilled this pastoral responsibility with high verbal and formal skill ("Nach den Worten der Prefatio soll die Dichtung dazu dienen, den Aberglauben zu bekämpfen und den *illiterati* das Christentum näher zu bringen. Der Dichter hat diese Aufgabe in christlichseelsorgerlichem Verantwortungsbewußtsein und mit höher sprachlicher und formaler Kunst gelöst") is inadequate but surely in the right direction. His additional comment that the *Heliand* author knew how to take into consideration, and build bridges to, the intellectual and spiritual situation of his people ("Er hat es verstanden, auf die geistige und religiöse Situation seiner Landsleute Rücksicht zu nehmen, ihnen Brücken zu bauen") can only be praised, but as an understatement![24]

Let us turn now to the question of the actual manuscripts of the *Heliand*. The text has come down to us today in two manuscripts, *M* (Munich, preserved in the Bavarian *Staatsbibliothek*) and *C* (Cotton Caligula AVIII, preserved in the British Museum) and in three fragments, *P* (formerly preserved in the University Library of Prague, now in Berlin), *V* (Codex Palatinus 1447, preserved in the Vatican), and *S* (the Straubing fragment, currently held in the Bavarian *Staatsbibliothek*). Scholars date *C* to the tenth century and *M* to the middle or late ninth century. Both derive from an earlier manuscript and are thus not the work of the poet-monk himself. *M* has generally been the preferred text since it is very close in time to the writing of the *Heliand* and is the most consistently Saxon. Rathofer and others prefer the later English manuscript *C*, on the grounds that it is far more faithful to the uncorrected inconsistencies of dialect of the presumed original and because it has preserved the original structural division of the *Heliand* into single chapter or song units called *fitts*.[25] Both *V* and *P* may be derived from two further sources, but there is no final unanimity among scholars on this point.[26]

The *Heliand* author was engaged in a highly original task. If he was in Fulda, there may have been a fairly large group of Frankish monks sitting not far from him in the scriptorium translating the four Gospels from the Latin version of *Tatian* into a literal, almost interlinear, form of their East Franconian dialect, the Old High German *Tatian*. It will be useful to contrast their work with his, since their task, though traditional and highly useful, is nowhere near as adventurous poetically as that set for himself by the Saxon monk who was composing the *Heliand*. The author was also using a Latin version of Tatian's *Diatessaron* 'through [the] Four', a harmony of the four Gospels of Matthew, Mark, Luke, and John, as the basis for his translation, but he was using it far more selectively and meditatively. He used the Bible commentaries of his time, especially Rabanus Maurus's commentary on Matthew, and he seems to have been familiar both with the legends and stories of the church as well as the epic tradition of the Saxons in Britain as in Cynewulf's *Crist*, to which tradition he shows a great kinship.[27]

Scholars of the *Heliand* have concentrated heavily on the text and language, comparison with Otfrid, problems of the place of origin, and the question of whether or not the *Heliand* represents an attempt to "accommodate" the Gospel. This latter thesis has been shown successfully by Rathofer, in his form study of the *C* manuscript, to be parallel to the hellenizing tendencies of Luke's Gospel. Rathofer's thorough and painstaking work on structure, however, seems not to have met with an enthusiastic acceptance,[28] indicating perhaps that there remains further need for study of the inner spirituality and pastoral orientation of the poetic hermeneutics of the *Heliand*—a study that does not rest primarily on a structural-mathematical analysis of the *fitts*. If the *praefatio* is correct, the task of the poet author was to *poetice transferre*. A proper study of the *Heliand* is one that treats it as an intercultural poetic translation of the Gospel created by an epic poet. Its anonymous author envisioned dynamic poetic equivalents so that the impact of the original text, in its Mediterranean cultural context, might be transferred by poetry analogously to a new North-Sea context. Such a task of inculturation had not been undertaken since the evangelists themselves.

Notes

1. From *Leges Saxonum und Lex Thuringorum* (Fontes Iuris Germanici Antiqui in usum Scholarum ex Monumentis Germaniae Historicis Separatim Editi). Ed. Claudius Freiherr von Schwerin. (Hannover and Leipzig: Hahnsche Buchhandlung, 1918), p. 40.

2. Cf. "Die Schriftheimat der Münchener Heliand-Handschrift" in *Beiträge zur Geschichte der deutschen Sprache und Literatur*, 101 (Tübingen, 1974), pp. 161 ff.

3. It is also curious *V* that one of the fragments of the *Heliand*, V, stems from Mainz. Rabanus went from Fulda to Mainz to be archbishop.

4. Achim Masser. *Bibel und Legendenepik des deutschen Mittelalters* (Berlin: Erich Schmidt Verlag, 1976), pp. 20–21.

5. *Bonifatii Epistolae: Willibaldi Vita Bonifatii*. Ed. Reinhold Rau (Darmstadt: Wissenschaftliche Buchhandlung, 1968), p. 494.

6. *Heliand und Genesis*. Herausgegeben von Otto Behaghel, 8. Auflage, bearbeitet von Walther Mitzka (Tübingen: Max Niemeyer Verlag, 1965), p. 5. Hereafter all citations will be given simply as chapter (song) and verse of the *Heliand*.

7. "In der alten germanischen Zeit hatte als Oberhaupt für den ganzen Stamm, wie schon bemerkt wird, nur im Fall eines Krieges ein Herzog an seiner Spitze gestanden" (Martin Lintzel, *Der sächsische Stammesstaat und seine Eroberung durch die Franken* [Berlin: Verlag Dr. Emil Ebering, 1933], p. 14).

8. I must disagree with Helmut de Boor. It seems incomprehensible to me that the term *drohtin* should by the year 830 already be a term exclusively restricted in Saxon to Christ. The local secular nobility had in no way ceased to exist; feudal lords and the ties of the *Gefolgschaft* did not disappear suddenly in the ninth century. The term "lord" in America, for example, has indeed suffered such a restrictive fate, since there are no secular lords here to designate as such, but I daresay the secular meaning of the term is alive and well in England where peers still abound. That *drohtin* in religious writings may have come to be the preferred term for Christ is no doubt true, but even in the literal Old High German *Tatian* there is the story of the servants and the talents (151, 5–7): two of the servants call the master *herro*, the other calls him

trohtin. Surely it is unwise to make such a judgement on the use of *drohtin* in the absence of secular literature which would be the place to make a decisive study on the secular survival of the term. Cf. Helmut de Boor, *Die deutsche Literatur von Karl dem Grossen bis zum Beginn der höfischen Dichtung* (Munich, C.H. Beck'sche Verlagsbuchhandlung, 1962), pp. 61–62.

9. Georgius Henricus Pertz, *Scriptores Rerum Germanicarum, Ex Monumentis Germaniae Historicis*, vol. 2 (Hannover: Hahn, 1865), pp. 9–10.

10. Einhard, *The Life of Charlemagne*, translated from *Monumenta Germaniae* by Samuel Epes Turner (Ann Arbor: University of Michigan Press, 1960), pp. 30–31.

11. G. Waitz, *Scriptores Rerum Germanicarum, Ex Monumentis Germaniae Historicis*, vol. 7 (Hannover: Hahn, 1883), pp. 44–48.

12. *Carolingian Chronicles: Royal Frankish Annals and Nithard's Histories*, trans. Bernard Walter Scholz with Barbara Rogers. (Ann Arbor: University of Michigan Press, 1972).

13. Waitz, *Scriptores*, p. 48.

14. Ibid., p. 52.

15. Both this excerpt and the following from the *Lex Salica* were noted in this context by Kurt Dietrich Schmidt in *Die Bekehrung der Germanen zum Christentum* (Göttingen: Vandenhoeck und Ruprecht, 1939), p. 179.

16. Waitz, *Scriptores*, pp. 60–63.

17. Ibid., p. 66.

18. Ibid., pp. 94–96.

19. Ibid., p. 118.

20. Georgius Henricus Pertz, *Nithardi Historiarum Libri III* in *Scriptores Rerum Germanicarum Ex Monumentis Germaniae Historicis*, vol. 6 (Hannover: Hahn, 1870), p. 13.

21. From Nithard's *Histories* in *Carolingian Chronicles*, p. 142.

22. Pertz, *Nithardi*, pp. 50 and 53.

23. Scholz, *Carolingian Chronicles*, pp. 170-173.

24. Heinz Rupp, "Der Heliand: Hauptanliegen seines Dichters" in Eichhoff and Rauch, *Der Heliand* (Darmstadt: Wissenschaftliche Buchgesellschaft, 1973), p. 269. (originally in *Der Deutschunterricht*, 8 (1956), Heft 1, pp. 28–45).

25. Cf. J. Rathofer, *Der Heliand: Theologischer Sinn als tektonische Form*; *Vorbereitung und Grundlegung der Interpretation*. (Cologne: Bohlau, 1962), passim.

26. Cf. Achim Masser, *Bibel*, pp. 19–20.

27. Cf. J. Knight Bostock, *A Handbook on Old High German Literature*, second edition revised by K. C. King and D. R. McLintock (Oxford: Clarendon Press, 1976), pp. 168–69.

28. Burkhard Taeger, in his Introduction to the ninth edition (1984) of Otto Behaghel's *Heliand und Genesis* comments that Rathofer's attempt to delineate a symbolic overall structure for the *Heliand* has failed, leaving only the possibility of seeing the work as a central composition organized around the Transfiguration. "Der Versuch, die Zahlung der Fittengliederung nicht nur als ursprünglich zu erweisen, sondern auch noch zahlen-symbolisch auszudeuten, ist gescheitert; übriggeblieben ist höchstens die Möglichkeit, den 'Heliand' als eine Zentralkomposition anzusehen, mit der Verklärung Christi auf dem Berg Tabor als in die Mitte des Werks gestellte, vorweggenommene Überwindung des Leidens" (Tübingen: Max Niemeyer Verlag, 1984), p. xx.

3
BIRTH AND DOOM

XIX. Similiter placuit his decretis inserere, quod omnes infantes infra annum baptizantur et hoc statuimus, ut si quis infantem intra circulum anni ad baptismum offere contempserit sine consilio vel licentia sacerdotis, si de nobile generi fuerit CXX solidos fisco conponat, si ingenuus LX, si litus XXX.

It has pleased us to insert into these decrees that all infants are to be baptized within one year [of birth]. This we have decreed so that if anyone should dare to refuse to present a child for baptism within its first year without the advice and consent of the priest, let him pay the following fine: if of the noble class, one hundred twenty solidi [if the solidus minor is meant, this is the equivalent of 60 head of cattle, if the solidus major is the fine, then 120 head of cattle] if a freeman, sixty; and if a bondsman, thirty. (Capitulatio de partibus Saxoniae, p. 40)

Despite the *Heliand* author's recurrent exhortation to his hearers to believe and not to doubt,[1] or perhaps because of the persistence of old images and concepts occasioning the doubt, he does not hesitate to incorporate the most profoundly pagan beliefs into his Gospel epic. Most surprising of all is his ability to find a place for *wurd*/Fate itself in this poem of the Gospel. In this the *Heliand* goes far beyond the hellenizing of St. Luke who gave no space to *moira*/Fate in the third Gospel.

Fate is first encoutered in the infancy narratives beginning with the prophecy of the birth of John the Baptist in the second song of the *Heliand*. The Angel Gabriel informs Zachary in the sanctuary of the temple that his son shall never in his life partake of wine or cider.

> That ni scal an is liƀa gio liđes anbitan wines an is weroldi: so haƀed im wurdgiscapu, metod gimarkod endi maht godes. [II, 127–129]
>
> *That never in his life will he drink cider or wine in this world: this is the way Fate made him, the Measurer marked him and the power of God [as well].*

The Latin *Tatian* simply has "vinum et siceram non bibit et spiritu sancto replebitur," and the literal Old High German *Tatian*: "win noh lid ni trinkit inti heilages geistes wirdit gefullit" (II, 6) [he will not drink wine or cider and he will be filled with the Holy Spirit].

Thus it seems that the private characteristics of a personality, the very attributes that the original describes as "to be filled with the Holy Spirit," came from other forces as well as from God. The *Heliand* author seems to have found a place for Fate and time (if not for Saxnot) within Christian theology. Like death in the later Middle Ages, which is imagined as a servant of God, Fate and time are treated almost as co-workers with God. John the Baptist's personal characteristics are given to him by a combination of his fatedness to be born in a given place and time and to be born of given persons, and by time or measure (which measures out to him the amount of his days and the time to his Fate) and by the power of God (or the Holy Spirit).[2] The word for God or Fate, *metod*, is related to the Old English *ge-met* and the modern German *Mass* 'measure'. It thus carries overtones of "that which is measured out to a man" and of God-the-measurer. The Greco-Roman image of the *Moirai* or *Parcae* with their thread might not be too far amiss here.

The word for Fate, *wrd* or *wurd*, is obviously related to the modern German *werden* 'to become', and perhaps less obviously but equally interestingly to the English word *weird*. Its primal meaning may have had to do with turning—the cosmic turning of the heavenly spheres that is related to time. This may be seen in *wurd*'s Latin relative *vertere* 'to turn'.

Though one could perhaps argue that the *Heliand* author is setting up here a new version of the Trinity (Fate, time, the power of God), I do not think this argument will stand and surely would defy his most obvious attempt to assert the primacy of non-doubting faith in Christ's paramount power. But the poet has room in his Christian poetic vision for godlike roles for both Fate and time. They are given charge of the "accidentals" of creation (what type of skin one will have, how tall one will be, which month—or whose sword—will carry one away, etc.). To God is left the absolute power of deciding to create and of altering these accidents if He so chooses (e.g., Christ's walking on the water) once Fate and time have done their subordinate tasks of accepting or rejecting a person after he has had his measure and met his Fate. Thus the coming-to-be, the *beginning* of the existence of John the Baptist, is not depicted as a shared responsibility of Fate, time, and God, but rather as the work of God alone:

> Tho warđ san aftar thiu maht godes, gicudid is craft mikel: warđ thiu quan ocan, idis an ira eldiu (III, 192–94)
>
> *Then, soon after, the power of God, his mighty strength, was revealed: the wife [Elizabeth] became pregnant, a woman in her old age*

The roles given to *wurd* and *metod* in the *Heliand* correspond to the roles given in modern theology to biological, physical, and socio-historical causes, and to coincidental, accidental events (Fate?) which modern theology and literature also attempt to cope with when dealing, for example, with the problem of evil or of suffering. The *Heliand* author could not sidestep the deepest level of Saxon religious consciousness and so found a niche for this ancient awareness.

The actual processes of John the Baptist's formation in the womb—biological processes—which are of little or no interest to evangelists or theologians, were safely attributed by the *Heliand* monk not to the Holy Spirit, but to Fate:

scolda im erƀiward,
suiđo godcund gumo gebiđig werden,
barn an burgun. Bed aftar thiu
that wif wurdigiscapu. Skred the wintar forđ,
geng thes geres gital. Iohannes quam
an liudeo lioht: lik was im sconi,
was im fel fagar, fahs endi naglos,
wangun warun im wlitige. (III, 194–201)

He [Zachary] would be given an heir, a very godlike man, [he would be given] a baby within the battlements. [Elizabeth] waited for this, the woman waited for what Fate was creating. Winter skidded by, the year wore on swiftly [metod?!], John came to the light of mankind: his body was beautiful, his skin was flawless as well as his hair and his nails, his cheeks shone.

We can see that the work of Fate in the womb of Elizabeth and *metod* in the passing of the nine months of time, have formed, in response to the will of God that John be, the body, complexion, perfect hair and nails of a most beautiful child. What an amazing contrast to the shaggy and unkempt John of traditional iconography! The child already shines with all the lightness and transparency that our author associates with divinity and with the kingdom of God. The *Heliand* appears to give God all ultimate power concerning the *bringing into existence* of persons and creatures, but leaves the detailed characteristics of the *essence* and the temporal *length of existence* of these persons to Fate and time. The result, stemming from belief in divine creation, is an early medieval correlation to the later Thomistic distinction between existence and essence with a rather dazzling combination of the two in the shining person of John the Baptist.

It goes without saying that the *Heliand* author must then see subsequent tragic events in John's life as the result of Fate and time rather than the direct and sole direction of God. The author is thus in a better position to explain the strange events of the death of John the Baptist without having to ask how the Christian God could be directly responsible for making such poor arrangements for the lives and destinies of his creatures. When John dies in the thirty-third song, there is no attempt to explain John's death as a result of Salome's dance and her mother's request; there is only mention of John's initial creation by the power of God:

Tho was endago allaro manno
thes wisoston thero the gio an thesa werold quami...
biutan so ine waldand god
fan heƀenwange helages gestes
gimarcode mahtig. (XXXIII, 2785–92)

That was the last day of the wisest of all men who ever came into this world...
but the Almighty God from the fields of heaven had marked him mightily by the Holy Spirit.

Here it seems that Fate and time, though powerful, rule, but with the adjunct power of almighty God's Holy Spirit.

A similar approach is seen in the parable of Lazarus and the rich man. When Lazarus's time to die comes in the forty-first song of the *Heliand*, our author says he heard that:

ina is reganogiscapu ...
gimanoda mahtiun suiđ, that he manno drom
ageƀen scolde. (XLI, 3347–50)

his sovereign Fate warned him quite mightily that he would have to give up the comings and goings of men.

Then the angels come and lead Lazarus off to the bosom of Abraham, but Fate also comes for the rich man:

Tho quamun ok wurdegiscapu,
themu odagan man orlaguile,[3]
that he thit lioht farlet: leđa wihti
besinkodun is siole an thene swarton hele
an that fern innen fiundun te willean,

begroƀun ine an gramono hem. (XLI, 3354-59)

Then the workings of Fate arrived also at the rich man, the fateful moment of truth when he left the light behind: evil creatures lowered his soul down to black Hel [herself],[4] *sank it into the inferno, just as the fiends desire, they buried him in that horrible homeland.*

Thus to Fate is conceded the role of warning, summoning, and determining the hour of death of humankind—together with the Spirit of God—in the *Heliand*. Only when the Heliand depicts Christ will incredible ingenuity be called for, since, as a human being, Jesus will be subject to the designs of implacable Fate, but as the Son of the Almighty, he will have to be depicted as being further beyond Fate's decisions than either Woden or Thor, both of whom in Germanic mythology are mortal divinities who are to die on the final day of doom.

To return to the more normal role of Fate, we can see further instances of Fate's role in the *Heliand* Gospel. When the Savior raises the dead child of the widow of Nain, the *Heliand* describes her plight:

it was ira enag barn:
siu was iru widowa, ne habda wunnea than mer,
biuten te themu enagun sunie al gelaten
wunnea endi willean, anttat ina iru wurd benam,
mari metodogescapu. [XXVI, 2186–90]

it was her only son: she was a widow, she had no more happiness, completely abandoned except for this one son, her pride and joy, until Fate took him from her, the Great Measurer's doings.

After following the standard account of Christ touching the bier and the young man being raised up and given back to his mother, the *Heliand* adds the following remark in the mother's statement to Christ. She falls at his feet and praises him, the *folco drohtin* 'clan lord', in front of the people:

Huand hie iro at so lioƀes ferahe mundoda wiđer metodigisceftie. (XXVI, 2209–10)

Since he had protected this life so dear to her against the measured workings of Fate.

The *Heliand* author's insertion clearly shows that his integration of Fate into the Gospel has also given him a means of verbalizing the extreme rank of the new god, Christ: he is able to alter the most irrevocable of the workings of Fate—death.

In the long interpretive discourse that our author allows himself in song forty-four, the blind man seated begging before the gates of Jericho is seen as a symbol of the human condition. In a passage that sounds almost reminiscent of Homer's description of mankind as like the passing generations of leaves on a tree,[5] the *Heliand* describes Jericho as named for the moon:

he ni mag is tidi bemiđen,
ac he dago gehuilikes duod ođerhueđer,
wanod ohtho wahsid. So dod an thesaro weroldi her,
an thesaro middilgard menniscono barn:
farad endi folgod, frode sterƀad,
werđad eft iunga aftar kumane,
weros awahsane, untat sie eft wurd farnimid. (XLIV, 3627-33)

he [the moon] cannot escape his orbit's time, thus on any given day he is either waning or waxing. That is what human beings do here in this world in this middle realm, the sons of men come and go in sequence, the old die, then the young who come after will wax older—until Fate removes them.

The curing of the blind thus is interpreted in the *Heliand* as an overcoming of our fated human condition here in the finite world of *middilgart*. The crying out of the blind man of Jericho is seen as the embodiment of the crying out of mankind to be released from the blindness of not knowing what was before or comes after, and from the recurring cycle of the life and death of each generation.

ac sie an waldand god
hludo hriopun, antat he im iro heli fargaf,
that sie sinlif gisehen mostin

open ewig lioht endi an faren
an thiu berhtun bu. (XLIV, 3650–54)

and they called out loudly to the ruling God, [asking] that he grant them healing so that they might be able to see eternal life, open, infinite light, and that they might be able to come to the bright shining building above.

One is reminded of the story (perhaps well known to the *Heliand* monk) recounted by the Venerable Bede of the conversion of King Edwin in 726 A.D. When he asked his counselors what they thought of the Christian religion, one of them touchingly described the human condition in the following manner:

"Talis," inquiens, "mihi uidetur, rex, uita hominum praesens in terris, ad conparationem eius, quod nobis incertum est, temporis, quale cum te residente ad caenam cum ducibus ac ministris tuis tempore brumali, accenso quidem foco in medio, et calido effecto caenaculo, furentibus autem foris per omnia turbinibus hiemalium pluuiarum uel niuium, adueniens unus passerum domum citissime peruolauerit; qui cum per unum ostium ingrediens, mox per aliud exierit. Ipso quidem tempore, quo intus est, hiemis tempestate non tangitur, sed tamen paruissimo spatio serenitatis ad momentum excurso, mox de hieme in hiemem regrediens, tuis oculis elabitur. Ita haec uita hominum ad modicum apparet; quid autem sequatur, quidque praecesserit, prorsus ignoramus. Unde si haec noua doctrina certius aliquid attulit, merito esse sequenda uidetur."[6]

"Your majesty, when you sit at table with your lords and vassals, in the winter when the fire burns warm and bright on the hearth and the storm is howling outside, bringing the snow and the rain, it happens of a sudden that a little bird flies into the hall. It comes in at one door and flies out through the other. For the few moments that it is inside the hall, it does not feel the cold, but as soon as it leaves your sight it returns to the dark of winter. It seems to me that the life of man is much the same. We do not

know what went before and we do not know what follows.
If the new doctrine can speak to us surely of these things,
it is well for us to follow it."[7]

Human temporariness and the human inability to see what is coming ten minutes from now, or next year, coupled with simultaneous awareness of the independently continuing sequence of events, produces a state of fear of the passage of time. Awareness of these realities, *metod* and *wurd*, is powerful in Germanic, and human, religious consciousness. It is indeed pointless for a poet-missionary to fight such awarenesses. Rather it is far better to acknowledge the place that they actually hold that seems to be the clear spiritual and methodological orientation of the *Heliand* monk. The *Heliand* author is no heretic or paganizing Saxon. He merely gives paganism its due, rendering unto Fate and time that which is theirs.[8] But he claims Christ can cure the blindness inherent in our being fated to a short span of life if we "call out loudly." This is surely not giving too much importance to Fate, but rather expresses in no uncertain Germanic terms just what the absolute power of the *waldand god* is.

The very weeping of Jesus over Jerusalem is reinterpreted by the *Heliand* to show that knowing the future events of the city is a characteristic of the One who presides over Fate.

we warđ thi, Hierusalem, quad he, thes thu te warun ni west
thea wurdegiskefti, the thi noh giwerden sculun,
huo thu noh wirđis behabd heries craftu (XLV, 3691–93)

Woe to you, Jerusalem, he said, that you truly don't know
the workings of Fate, which are going to happen to you,
how you are going to be surrounded by a powerful army...

This seems such an obvious passage for a reference to Fate that it is important to note that no such reference is made in the Old High German *Tatian*, which translates literally from the Latin:

oba forstuontistu inti giwesso in thesemo thinemo tage
thiu dar thir zi subbu sint. (116,6)

si cognovisses et tu et quidem in hac die tua quae ad pacem tibi sunt.

if [only] you understood, and truly in this your day, those things that are for your peace.

Not only is there no thought of mentioning Fate, there is not even a "Woe!" For the *Heliand* poet not only gives Christ his Gospel due, but he also may be protecting himself from fellow monks of the more Bonifacian school by ingeniously finding an acknowledgment of the powerful existence of Fate and doom in the original Gospel account itself. Should anyone object on the grounds of religious orthodoxy to the presence of *wurd* and *metod* in a Christian epic, our author has pointed out that Christ himself foresaw the Fate that was to overtake Jerusalem: Christ himself gave adequate acknowledgment of the effectiveness of the workings of Fate when he wept over Jerusalem, foretelling in 33 A.D. her bloody fate a generation later at the hands of the tenth legion. And what monk would deny what Christ acknowledged?!

The *Heliand* author inserts Fate where circumstances have brought misfortune. Even the most unfortunate event of all, the last day of an individual, or of all mankind, is expressed in traditional northern terms. In the well-known story of the raising of Lazarus, Martha replies to Christ's statement "your brother will rise again," with "I know that he will rise again *on the last day*." In *Tatian*'s Latin this is: "scio quia resurget in resurrectione in novissima die," which in the Old High German *Tatian* is "ih weiz thaz her erstentit in theru urresti *in themo iungisten tage*," (135,14), and becomes in the *Heliand*:

All hebbiu ik giloƀon so . . .,
that he than fan erđu scal up astanden
an themu domes daga. (XLIX, 4045–49)

That is what I completely believe, that he will rise up from the earth on doomsday.

Thomas the Apostle even refers to the coming death of Christ as Christ's doom (XLVIII, 3998) in a startling statement not much ameliorated by having the apostles be fatefully doomed to desert their clan-lord (LIX, 4931–4936) and to have it foretold by their clan-lord himself.

The birth of John the Baptist clearly introduces the note of Fate in the *Heliand*. Let us turn now to the infancy narrative of the birth of Christ.

The annunciation to Mary and the incarnation of the second Person of the Trinity are described in the Fourth song of the *Heliand*. This account appears to have erred, not so much in the direction of over-germanizing, but rather in the direction of a mistaken overorthodoxy. In response to Mary's question to the Angel Gabriel: "How shall this be, for I have not known man?", the angel replies:

An thi scal helag gest fon hebanwange
cuman thurh craft godes. Thanan scal this kind odan
werđan an thesaro weroldi. Waldandes craft
scal thi fon them hohoston hebancuninge
scadowan mid skimon. Ni warđ scionera giburd
ne so mari mid mannun, huand siu kumid thurh maht godes
an these widen werold. (IV, 275–80)

Scott translates:

From the meadows of sky the Holy Ghost shall descend through the strength of God. From Him will a Wee One be granted thee here in this world. The Wielder's strength will o'ershadow thee, the Heaven-King All High with his shade. Below was never a birth so fair. Never so wondrous among men. For from God's might It cometh here to this world. (p. 9)

The most remarkable aspect of the passage is not a statement as much as an omission. There is no mention of Fate whatsoever. As would be expected, the birth of Christ will be strictly through the overshadowing power of God. There is no mention, however, of the human body of the incarnate God, as there was so conspicuously in the case of the complexion, hair, and fingernails of John the Baptist, presumably because that would elicit questions in the hearers' minds as to who arranged the color of hair and other physical characteristics of Christ. The *existence* of Christ is attributed to the power, the Spirit of God.

The *essence* and Fate of Christ are glossed over lest *wurd* and *metod* surface in the consciousness of the audience and be given some credit for the coming of Christ. The author cannot resist mentioning, as he did with John the Baptist, how *beautiful* this birth is: Ni ward scionera giburd (IV, 279) 'Never was there a more beautiful birth'. But the beauty specifically refers to the event, not the person, and the beauty is attributed to the power of God, not to the workings of Fate in the womb.

Mary's consent is left unaltered, but expanded to include the author's own constant message to the Saxons, "don't doubt":

> werđe mi aftar thinun wordun, al so is willeo si, herron mines; nis mi hugi tuifli ne word ne wisa. (IV, 286–288)
>
> *Be it done unto me according to your word, whatever should be the will of my lord; my heart and mind are not in doubt, neither in word nor in deed.*

The *Heliand* poet then tells of the incarnation, announcing it with the old epic introductory line, *So gifragn ik* 'I have heard it told'. He continues praising with what good faith *'mid gilobon godon,'* light-hearted mind *'mid leohtu hugi'* and transparent loyalty *'mid hluttrun trewn'* Mary accepted the proposal. This is followed by a shocking turn of phrase: Warđ the helago gest that barn an ira bosma (IV, 291–92) 'The Holy Spirit became the child in her womb'. This surely exceeds the *et incarnatus est de Spiritu Sancto ex Maria Virgine* formula of the creed of Nicea. In orthodox theological terms, it is the second Person of the Trinity, the Son, who becomes man in Jesus Christ, not the first Person, the Father, nor the third Person, the Holy Spirit. It has to be admitted that the *Heliand* does exhibit the anti-Arian, docetist bias of its time, but to say that the *Holy Spirit*, not the Son, is the child of Mary's womb is simply a blunder that exceeds all that is even required for good docetism. Though he may have made a serious mistake here—one could be invaluable for finding his source in a defective copy of the Nicean creed—the author's intent is made all the more clear by the mistake.

In contrast to the birth of John the Baptist, the existence of the Savior is thus described as an utterly divine event, with no terrestrial or cosmic admixture of the workings of weird Fate. This surely confirms Göhler's thesis against Vilmar, for not only is the incarnation the work of the Holy Spirit alone, the whole being in Mary's womb is *of* the Holy Spirit. Unfortunately our author goes one step further and says it *is* the Holy Spirit. In this declaration the *Heliand* author is misled by his great effort to establish both the difference and the superiority of Christ to Woden and Thor, whose "divine" origin and birth were entirely *within* the world from cosmic natural forces, thus being subjects of both time and Fate as ultimate deciders of all world events. The *Heliand* insists that Christ is from heaven above, from "the meadows of the sky," and his origin lies in the all-ruling God and the strength (Spirit) of God. The author's intent is surely to say that Jesus Christ is the transcendent strength (Spirit) of God come into the world to rescue those who have faith and "do not doubt, neither in word nor in deed."

The very structural rearrangement of this scene makes his intent clear. The sequence of events in *Tatian* (III-V) is as follows:

1. Annunciation to Mary—the incarnation
2. Visitation of Mary to Elizabeth
3. Birth of John the Baptist
4. The book of the family tree of Christ
5. Joseph's doubt and faith.

The structure in the *Heliand* has been greatly simplified and pointed:

1. Annunciation to Mary, who reacts with no doubt, but faith
2. Incarnation of the Holy Spirit
3. Annunciation to Joseph, who reacts with doubt, then faith.

The visitation and the "begats" of the family tree of Jesus have been excised completely, the birth of John the Baptist removed to the earlier song, leaving us with a balanced framework, the incarnation in the middle, Mary and Joseph on either side, thus allowing the angel who announces to Mary to be balanced by the angel who explains to Joseph. Joseph's initial doubt and his subsequent faith are already in the original account and thus the author had only to add a reference to doubt and faith in Mary's reaction to the incarnation ("my heart and mind are not in doubt, neither in word nor in deed") to form a magnificent symmetry out of the latent balance in the arrangement of the original accounts. The author liked triptychs.

Fate does manage to find a place for itself, however. Song four relegates Fate to the position of being the messenger when the time has come. Almost as though the pregnancy of Mary were too sublimely spiritual for her to notice it, she has to be reminded by Fate when the time has come for her to give birth. In MS *M* the word *godes* 'God's' appears before *giscapu* 'Fate', thus appearing to make Fate a messenger of God's will. In MS *C*, which seems to many to be closer in fidelity if not in age to the original lost MS, the word *godes* is not found:

endi siu so subro drog
al te huldi godes helagna gest,
godlican gumon, antat sie [godes] giscapu
mahtig gimanodun, that siu in an manno lioht,
allaro barno bezt, brengean scolda. (IV, 334–38)

And she carried so clearly—all for the glory of God—the Holy Spirit, the divine man, until [God's] Fate-workings admonished her mightily that she should bring him to the light of humankind, the best son ever born.

In emphasizing Christ's sovereign status above normal Fate-workings, our author does not forget his audience. David's *burg*, Bethlehem, is deftly moved to *Germania* and the story is told:

Thar gifragn ic, that si thiu berhtun giscapu,
Marium gimanodun endi maht godes,
that iru an them siđa sunu odan warđ ,

giboran an Bethleem barno strangost,
allaro cuningo craftigost ...

Tho was it all giwarod so,
so it er spaha man gisprocan habdun,
thurh huilic odmodi he thit erđriki herod
thurh is selƀes craft sokean welda,
managaro mundboro. Tho ina thiu modar nam,
biwand ina mid wadiu wiƀo sconiost,
fagaron fratahun, endi ina mid iro falmon tuuem
legda lioƀlico luttilna man
that kind an ena cribbiun, thoh he habdi craft godes,
manno drohtin. Thar sat thiu modar biforan,...
held that helaga barn: ni was ira hugi twifli...

wardos antfundun
thea thar ehuscalcos uta warun,
weros an wahtu, wiggeo gomean,
fehas aftar felda: gisahun finistri an twe
telatan an lufte, endi quam lioht godes
wanum thurh thiu wolcan endi thea wardos thar
befeng an them felda. (V, 367–93)

I have heard it told, that the shining workings
[of Fate] and the power of God told Mary
that on this site a son would be granted her,
born in Bethlehem, the strongest child, the most
powerful of all kings ...

There it all came to pass, just as wise men,
long ago, had said: that he would come in humility,
by his own power, to visit the realm of earth,
He who is the ruler of multitudes. Then his mother
took him, that most beautiful woman, wrapped Him in
clothes
and precious jewels, then with her two hands laid him
gently, the little man, that child, in a [fodder-] crib,
even though he had the power of God, the liege-lord of
mankind. There the mother sat in front of him ...
she held the holy child: nor was her mind in doubt ...

The guards heard [the news], as grooms they were outside, men on guard duty, watching over the horses—the beasts of the field: they saw the darkness split in two in the sky, and the light of God came shining through the clouds and surrounded the guards there on the field.

In this retelling of the Christmas story our author has included, in miniature, many of his major themes and devices (except that of the frame or *inclusio*). He singles out the importance of the event by beginning again, in the middle of the song, with the ancient formula *thar gifragn ic* 'I have heard it told' and then has not only the power of God but also the workings of Fate inform Mary that this is the place for the birth of her powerful son.

The emphasis on the intrinsic strength of Christ is, I believe, sufficiently recurrent to merit a closer look. Two *loci* where the meaning of this emphasis may best be explored are here in the nativity account and in the incident of Christ walking on the water. In the nativity scene above we are told explicitly that he came down from heaven to the earthly kingdom by means of *is selƀes craft* (V, 377) 'his own power.' When Christ comes toward the apostles across the Lake of Galilee, we are told that he held himself up from sinking into the water strictly by *is selƀes craft* (XXV, 2922). Both phrases are the author's own insertion and are his own phrasing. They are consistent with his view of the incarnation as being that of the Holy Spirit rather than the Son, but once more I believe we can discern his purpose. The Saxons, as well as other northern Germanic peoples in the next centuries, were still torn between Thor and Woden on the one side and "the mighty Christ" on the other.

Thor was known for his strength but, even in his great strength as a mortal god, he needed magic devices to help him rule sea storms and overcome his enemies in the world of cosmic nature. It was known to all what he could do with his hammer—a symbol of his power that was worn as an amulet even by converts to Christianity. More important was Woden's ability both to descend and ascend the *bifrost*, the Milky Way, and thus be able to come from above and visit the realm of men and to go in seven-league strides across the face of the sea. These feats, however, he accomplished only by having the help of *Sleipnir*, the giant eight-legged cosmic horse of ancient mythology.[9] How seriously the Saxons took this part of their mythology cannot be said with accuracy, but they certainly did not abandon it quickly or gladly, no doubt precipitating the *Heliand* poet's efforts to compare Christ's power with that of Thor and Woden: Christ also came down from heaven, walked on water and calmed storms. But he did all these by *is selƀes craft*.

As to the scandal of the nonnoble birth circumstances, our author does as well as he can. The placing of Christ in the animals' food trough is not denied, but it is made both more warmly human and almost sacramental by distracting the hearer to Mary's gentle hands and her reverential treatment of the child. The author does not flee from the paradox of the mighty God in such low estate, but keeps reminding the hearer that this "little man" is the "liege-lord of Mankind." He inserts his constant admonition to the Saxons: Mary saw all this and she did not doubt.

There are a few details our author cannot face, however, or that he thinks might be too much for the Saxons: the swaddling clothes and the shepherds' sheep. The swaddling clothes in *Tatian* are quite clear: "et pannis eum involvit / inti biwant inan mit tuochum" (V, 6 and 13) [and she wrapped him in cloths]; they are changed in the *Heliand* to clothes and jewels, Joseph becomes a noble Saxon whose grooms are outside watching the horses, and it is to them that the angels sing on Christmas Eve. Sheep could not have been totally unknown among people who wore woolen clothing; therefore, the reason for the change to horses and squires must be to assure the Saxons of Joseph's higher rank.

More telling than these changes, from a human viewpoint, is the total elimination of what must be the saddest line in the nativity narrative—"for there was no room for them in the inn." Perhaps our author thought it simply too much to accept that the Christian God could be depicted as descending from the meadows of heaven to *middlegard*, and find here no welcome. Perhaps the ancient rules of hospitality and the hallowed traditions of *Gastfreundschaft* were seen as so inviolable (witness *Beowulf*) that the author thought his audience could not accept that such poor treatment could happen to a god and go unavenged by heaven. Significantly for our appreciation of the sensitivities of his time, the author leaves this part of the story out of his document. To hear something of the sadness of what it might have sounded like, we must go to the literal translation of the Old High German *Tatian*. In this account Mary and Joseph poignantly meet the fate of common travelers: "im ni was ander state in themo gasthuse" (V,13) [there was no other place for them in the inn]. According to the sensibilities of the *Heliand* author, this could not have been how Joseph and his retinue were received in Fort David.

Respect for the customs and knowledge of Teutonic peoples is shown in the author's approach to the wisdom of the pagans and barbarians. The story of the coming of the wise men from the East provides the *Heliand* an opportunity for a long and inventive exercise. This is the obvious place for him to justify his own effort to accept foreign religious values into the Christian message since the story of the wise men points out that there were foreigners far from the purview of Judaeo-Christian revelation who could read God's "spell" in the skies and come to the correct lord at the correct time seeking to find him. The *Heliand* devotes two full songs to the coming of the wise men, twice as much as is given to the nativity itself. The first of these, song seven, is of interest to us here.

Song seven balances the workings of Fate in determining the physical shape of John the Baptist and even the circumstances of Christ's birth, by asserting quite plainly that the non-Christian wise men were driven by God's fateful workings *'dribun im godes giscapu'* (547). This would have been welcome philosophy to the Irish monks, who had expressed their Christianity in their non-romanized Celtic culture, and to Rabanus Maurus, abbot of Fulda at the time the *Heliand* was most probably written. In response to Herod's astonished question as to why such well-born men should have come from so far to his kingdom, the three tell him that many wise old men in the East had promised that help would one day come from heaven. In particular, they describe a man from the East in ancient times, their ancestor, a man of such knowledge that he *mahte rekkian spel godes* 'he could figure out the message of God' (572). The barely disguised play on *spel godes* and *godes spel* 'gospel' is hard to overlook. If the wise men's great ancestor in the pagan East was able to recognize God's spell in the skies, the Saxons should be able to do it too; and a poet who uses the wisdom of his pagan ancestors to *rekkian spel godes* is not doing an unholy or un-Christian thing, but merely following the path of the wise men who also came to Christ by following the astrological wisdom of their ancestors.

The *Heliand* author further elaborates his internal *apologia* for his own work by imagining a death scene for this far distant ancestor of the wise men. Being told that he will soon have to leave the comings and goings of men *'liudio drom'* to go to the other light *'sokien liohtođar'*, he calls his disciples around him and makes his final statement to them, a prophecy of the future.[10] Though the author may have been thinking possibly of Zoroaster, and was apparently using Old Testament structures to create this scene, he seems clearly to have intended that his hearers think of their Germanic ancestors and imagine—correctly or incorrectly—that *they* had foretold the coming of the Savior. This is seen in the evocative vocabulary in which *middilgard* is used twice in solemn fashion for earth, and even in the first words where *tho sagda he* commences the prophetic saga instead of the more common *tho quadhe*:

tho sagda he that her scoldi cuman en wiscuning
mari endi mahtig an thesan middilgard
thes bezton giburdies; quađ that it scoldi wesan barn
godes,
quađ that he thesero weroldes waldan scoldi
gio te ewandaga, erđun endi himiles.
He quađ that an them selbon daga, the ina saligna
an thesan middilgard modar gidrogi
so quađ he that ostana en scoldi skinan
himiltungal huit, sulic so wi her ne habdin er
undartuisc erđa endi himil ođar huerigin
ne sulic barn ne sulic bocan. (VII, 582–92)

Then he spoke and said there would come a wise king,
magnificent and mighty, to this middle realm; he would
be of the best birth; he said that he would be the Son of
God,
he said that he would rule this world,
earth and sky, always and forevermore.

he said that on the same day on which
the mother gave birth to the Blessed One in this middle
realm, in the East, he said, there would shine forth
a brilliant light in the sky, one such as we never had
before between heaven and earth nor anywhere else,
never such a baby and never such a beacon.

Though Fate and its foretelling are not explicitly mentioned, the whole repetitive form bespeaks a creative mentality that respects a preplanned future as a matter of inevitable fact.

In dealing with the death of Christ, the *Heliand* has a sovereign opportunity to express the old teaching that Christ gave himself up of his own free will. Having shown in the stories of the raising of the son of the widow of Naim and of Lazarus that the mighty Christ is above the decisions of *wurd*/Fate and can even reverse Fate's decision if he so chooses, the author shows that Christ, in his own case, is letting the decision on the length of his own life be settled by *wurd*/Fate. When the high priest asks the Sanhedrin what their decision is with regard to Christ, the *Heliand* has him say: *Huat williad gi Iudeon thes/adelien te dome?* (LX, 5104–5) 'What judgment of doom do you Jews wish for this man?' *Tatian* represents this as: *Waz thunkit iuwich?* (191,2) 'What do you think?' What man, in his own case, having power to reverse the fateful events of this world would voluntarily hand that power over to a hostile Sanhedrin—unless he could overcome his doom even after death.

The poet has Christ concealing his divinity from the people in the scene before Pilate out of fear that, if they knew who Christ was, they would not dare harm him; thus the kingdom of heaven would not be unlocked to the sons of men. As Barabbas approaches, our author cannot but add ominously, *Thiu wurd nahida thuo* 'Fate was coming closer then'. Yet he hastens to add in modification, *mari maht godes* 'the great power of God' and proceeds to an allusion to *metod*/time—*endi middi dag* (LXIV, 5394–96) 'and midday', the time when Jesus was to begin his three hours of agony on the cross.

In the case of Jesus, the *Heliand* author finally and clearly makes Fate not just a servant force of God but his divine power.

Doubtless this is because he did not feel at ease, even temporarily, to allow the ultimate pagan force to overcome the mighty Christ. The deceptively simple phrase "Fate was coming closer" expresses eloquently that, on an emotional level, the old fear of *wurd*/Fate is still present and that *mari maht godes* is more a solution the author seems led to rather than one he enjoys. How he was led to these choices may be seen in his casting of Satan in the role of one who dons a cloak of invisibility (a common device in Germanic mythology) so as to work against Christ's being doomed to crucifixion. It is Satan who gave Pilate's wife the tormenting dream so that she pleaded with her husband to have nothing to do with this just man. This is portrayed as Satan's scheme so that the gates of hell would remain intact and open, and heaven's kingdom would remain closed to men. Seen in this light, the only being who fought against Christ's approaching Fate was Satan, who saw it as a threat to his own kingdom. If Satan viewed Christ's impending Fate as threatening, our author can say that Christ's Fate came from God directly "to save us all from Satan's power when we were gone astray."

Notes

1. Cf. Heinz Rupp, "Der Heliand: Hauptanliegen seines Dichters," *Der Deutschunterricht*, 8 (1956), Heft 1, p. 28.

2. Cf. Samuel Berr, *An Etymological Glossary to the Old Saxon Heliand* (Bern and Frankfurt: Herbert Lang, 1971), pp. 278–79, 438 and 463. Also Ladislaus Mittner, *Wurd: das Sakrale in der altgermanischen Epik* (Bern: Francke Verlag, 1955), pp. 82ff.

3. The word *orlaguile* is an impressive composite for the moment of Fate or destiny. In modern German it might be *Urlagezeit*, paraphrased in English perhaps as "the time of the way things really are." *Or* means primeval, basic, root; *lag* is situation or place, and *huile* (while) is moment or time.

4. Hel is the old Germanic goddess of the dead in the underworld, parallel to Pluto in Greco-Roman mythology. The *Heliand* elicits both the pagan Nordic image of hell by referring to Hel and the fiery Mediterranean-Christian one by referring to it as *fern*, from the Latin *infernum*.

5. Iliad, VI, 146.

6. *Venerabilis Bedae Opera Historica*, ed. Carolus Plummer (Oxford: Clarendon Press, 1961), p. 112.

7. *Bede's Ecclesiastical History of the English People*, ed. Bantam Colgrove and R.A.B. Mynors (Oxford: Clarendon Press, 1969), book 2, chap. 13, pp. 183–85.

8. This poetic parallelism of thought between Bede's story of the conversion of the king and the *Heliand* poet's interpretation of the blind man seems to me more apparent than either Krogmann's attempt to reject the passage as a later insertion or Rathofer's attempt to attribute it to the *Heliand* poet's mere use of Rabanus's and Bede's Gospel commentaries. Cf. their heated dispute in Johannes Rathofer, "Zum Aufbau des Heliand" in Eichhoff and Rauch, *Der Heliand* (Darmstadt: Wissenschaftliche Buchgesellschaft, 1973), pp. 380–85 (originally in *Zeitschrift für deutsches Altertum*, 93 (1964), pp. 239–72).

9. Cf. H.R. Ellis Davidson, *Gods and Myths of Northern Europe* (Harmondsworth: Penguin Books, 1964), p. 26.

10. I do not know if the author is alluding to Zoroaster, as may perhaps be implied. I think it more likely that he is simply

taking the general structure of the many Old Testament death scenes (e.g., the death of Joseph in Egypt) and then inventing his story around the structure using Germanic imagery. The general formal structure of this literary form of the death scene in the Old Testament might be summarized as (1) main character on the point of death summons his followers to say goodbye, often at bedside; (2) he exhorts them to continue his tradition and blesses them; (3) he makes a (lengthy) prophecy of the future. Cf. Xavier Leon DuFour, S.J., "Jesus' Understanding of His Death," *Theology Digest*, 24, 3 (Fall 1976), pp. 295–96.

4

PETER'S LONGBOAT

XXXIV. Interdiximus, ut omnes Saxones generaliter conventus publicos nec faciant, nisi forte missus noster de verbo nostro eos congregare fecerit.

It is prohibited for the Saxons in general to hold any public assemblies, unless by chance our delegate should, on our word, have them come together. (Capitulatio de partibus Saxoniae, p. 43)

The crucial figure of Peter is first presented to the reader in the fourteenth song of the *Heliand*, as Christ leaves behind his period of forty days in the desert and begins his public ministry:

> Was im an them sinweldi salig barn godes
> lange huile, unthat im tho liođora warđ
> that he is craft mikil cuđien wolda
> weroda te willion. Tho forlet he waldes hleo,
> enodies ard endi sohte im eft erlo gemang,
> mari meginthiode endi manno drom...
> He began in samnon tho
> gumono te iungaron, godoro manno
> wordspaha weros. (XIV 1121–26, 1148–50)

For a long while then, God's blessed Bairn
dwelt in the wilderness,
Till it seemed to Him better for the benefit of all
That he show His great strength to the folk. Thus he
forsook the shade of the forest, the spot in the wood,
And again He did seek the company of earls
The illustrious thanes and the throngs of men...
he began to gather together
Youths for disciples, young men and good,
Word-wise warriors. (Scott, pp. 37-38)

Christ is depicted here as a Germanic chieftain gathering young noblemen to be in his private retinue. The wilderness of the Judean desert is turned into a northern forest. Christ can thus be envisaged as a Germanic lord leaving "the shade of the forest" to gather these clan warriors for battle. This scene closely corresponds with the pastoral intent of the author of the Heliand who may have seen himself writing this epic precisely to gather and convert "youths for disciples, young men and good, word-wise warriors" (not sword-wise!):

Geng im tho bi enes wateres stađe,
thar thar habda Iordan aneban Galileo land
enna se gewarhtan. Thar he sittean fand
Andreas endi Petrus bi them ahastrome,
beđea thea gebrođar thar sie an bred watar
swiđo niudlico netti thenidun
fiscodun im an them flode. Thar sie that fridubarn godes
bi thes sees stađe selbo grotta.
(XIV, 1150–57)

He went to the shores of a water
there where the Jordan had spread to a sea
on the border of Galilee-land. There he saw sitting
Andrew and Peter; found the two by the flowing water.
The brothers both down by the broad stream
were very neatly throwing their nets,
fishing in the flood. There first the Peace Bairn of God
himself did greet them on the shores of the sea.
(Scott, p. 38)

The author is very concerned with the landscape of this scene. He repeatedly emphasizes the site at which the calling of the disciples took place. Once he has demonstrated his accurate geographic knowledge of the Jordan as spreading to form the Sea of Galilee, he repeats "there by the water" again and again in the manner of a preacher, slowly blending the Sea of Galilee with the North Sea. A quick glance at *Tatian* will show how much he has elaborated this one aspect of the original:

> Ambulans autem juxta mare Galileae vidit duos fratres, Simonem qui vocatur Petrus et Andreas fratem ejus, mittentes vete in mare, erant enim piscatores / Ganganti nah themu sevvu Galilee gisah zwene bruoder, Simonem, thie giheizan ist Petrus, into Andream sinan bruoder, sententi iro nezzi in seo, wanta sie warun fiscara. (*Tatian* 19, 1)

The emphasis in the original is on the fact that the two brothers were fishermen. The emphasis in the *Heliand* is on the fact that the calling to discipleship took place *thar* ... *bi thes sees stađe* 'there... by the shores of the sea'—just where the poet's listeners were.

The author insists on the locale by repetition and saxonizes it with a rich diversity of local seashore vocabulary: *bi enes wateres stađe*; *enna se*; *bi them aha* (cf. "aqua") *strome*; *an bred watar*; *an them flode*; *bi thes sees stađe*.

To counteract the coming of Christianity to Saxony by the sword, the *Heliand* depicts Christ as coming to the land where the rivers widen to the sea as the *fridubarn godes*, God's child of peace. Gently he emphasizes in the last line that he personally (*selbo*) has come to speak to them. Throughout this song, as each disciple is called to join Christ's retinue, the author reminds the listener that it happened by the water:

> forletun al saman
> Andreas endi Petrus, so hwat so sie bi theru ahu habdun,
> gewunstes [C has gewunnanes] bi them watare.
> (XIV, 1165–67)

They abandoned at once,
Andrew and Peter, everything they had by the sea, what-
ever they had come to own
by the water's edge

Once again the emphasis on water, which is repeated (*aha* and *watar*) is the author's own. He also specifies that leaving behind one's possessions in order to become a member of the Lord's retinue, a liegeman of the Savior, is eminently worthwhile. In order to underscore this point, he explains it directly to his audience in the last three lines of the following:

was im willeo mikil,
that sie mid them godes barne gangen mostin,
samad an is gisiđea scoldun saliglico
lon antfahan: so dot liudeo so hwilic,
so thes herran wili huldi githionon,
gewirkean is willeon. (XIV, 1167–72)

There was a powerful desire in them
that they had to go with the Son of God,
as a part of his retinue, that they should blessedly
receive their reward: that is what everyone does
who wishes to do this lord's will and intent,
to carry it out.

It may be overly didactic, but the author gives away his intent so that the listener might identify with Peter as he is portrayed, and follow Peter's example. James and John go in the same manner, though they leave even more behind:

tho sie bi thes wateres stađe
furđor quamun, tho fundun sie thar enna frodan man
sittean bi them sewa endi is sunni twene
Iacobus endi Iohannes: warun im iunga man.
Satun im tha gesunfader an enumu sande uppen,
brugdun endi bottun beđium handun
thiu netti niudlico, thea sie habdun nahtes er
forsliten an them sewa. Thar sprac im selƀo to
salig barn godes, het that sie an thana siđ mid im

Iacobus endi Iohannes, gengin beđie,
kindiunge man. Tho warun im Kristes word
so wirđig an thesaro weroldi, that sie bi thes watares stađe
iro aldan fader enna forletun,
frodan bi them flode, endi al that sie thar fehas ehtun,
nettiu endi neglitskipu, gecuran im thana neriandan Krist,
helagna te herron, was im is helpono tharf
te githiononne: so is allaro thegno gehwem,
wero an thesaro weroldi. (XIV, 1172–89)

As they went along
the shores of the water, they met a sage
sitting by the sea and his sons twain
Jacob and John, young men on the Jordan,
sons and father, they sat on the sands;
Neatly they knotted and mended their nets
with both their hands, the nets which the night before
they had slit in the sea. Then He spoke to them;
God's Blessed Bairn bade them be on their way now with him.
Jacob and John, they both did go,
The child-young men. Christ's word was for them
so worthy here in this world, that on the shores of the water
they forsook their father above by the flood,
the ancient alone, and all that they owned,
their nets and well-nailed ships. They chose All-Nurturing Christ,
Holy Savior and Lord. To earn His help
was the need they felt. So feel all thanes,
all warriors here in this world. (Scott, pp. 38–39)

As they are called, "sitting on the sand," they leave even their father behind—something taken directly from the Gospel itself. What the author adds are the nailed northern ships and the sand dunes. It is not too far a leap to see that, by joining Peter's retinue, one becomes a member of the North-Sea knight companions of Christ.

Further along, as the author describes Matthew leaving his counting table, he is made the Lord's knight, welcome in Christ's mead hall:

endi ward im uses drohtines man;
cos im the cuninges thegn Crist te herran
milderan medomgebon, than er is mandrohtin
wari an thesero weroldi... [XIV, 1198–1201]

And he [Matthew] became our Lord's man;
the royal warrior chose for himself Christ as his lord,
a more generous mead giver than he had ever had before
as a liege lord in this world.

In today's more sober world we may be a little surprised to see the term for a benevolent king or nobleman—"generous mead giver"—applied to Christ. The *Heliand* monk might respond that there was a parallel element of divine generosity in the matter of alcohol at the wedding feast of Cana when Jesus turned water rather abundantly into wine.

The assembling of the apostles in the fourteenth song of the *Heliand* appears to have a triadic structure: first, the calling of Peter and Andrew from their boats and nets by the water's edge; second, the calling of James and John from their well-nailed boats and their aged father; and, third, the calling of 'noble' Matthew who changes lords and becomes the King's man, entitled to his liege lord's generosity. The structure is an upward moving one with the emphasis on material possessions, livelihood, and persons left behind in the first and second instances, moving to awareness of what is gained in the third instance. The author makes no personal comment after the calling of Peter and Andrew, makes a brief personal interjection after that of James and John, and a more extended one after the 'noble thane' Matthew accepts the invitation, thus helping to mark the ascending sequence in their responses from acceptance, to departure, to meadhall friendship with the Lord.

The *Heliand* author's concentration on the figure of Peter the fisherman is remarkably developed in the masterful scene when Jesus and Peter are walking on the water (XXXV). The original version of the incident found in the *Diatessaron* (chap. 81) harmonizes the relevant verses of Matthew 14, Mark 6, and John 6 as follows:

> Vespere autem facto solus erat ibi. Navicula autem in medio mari iactabatur fluctibus; erat enim contrarius ventus. Quarta autem vigilia noctis videns eos laborantes venit ad eos ambulans supra mare et volebat preterire eos. Et videntes eum supra mare ambulantem turbati sunt dicentes, quod fantasma est, et pre timore clamaverunt. Statimque Ihesus locutus est eis dicens: habete fiduciam, ego sum, nolite timere. Respondens autem Petrus dixit: domine, si tu es, iube me venire ad te super aquas. At ipse ait: veni! Et descendens Petrus de navicula ventum validum timuit, et cum coepisset mergi, clamavit dicens: domine, salvum me fac! Et continuo Ihesus extendens manum apprehendit eum et ait illi: modice fidei, quare dubitaste? Et cum ascendissent in naviculam, cessavit ventus, et statim fuit navis ad terram quam ibant. Qui autem in navicula erant, venerunt et adoraverunt eum dicentes: vere filius dei es.
>
> *When evening came he was alone there. The boat, however, was in the middle of the sea being tossed about by the waves: the wind was against them. At the fourth watch of the night [3 A.M. to dawn] Jesus, seeing them struggling, came to them, walking on the water as if he wanted to pass them by. Seeing him walking on the water they became agitated and said that it was a ghost, and began to scream out of fear. Suddenly Jesus spoke to them and said, "Be confident, it is me, do not be afraid." Peter answered and said, "Lord, if it is you, tell me to come to you across the waters." And he said, "Come." Then Peter got off the boat and was walking on the water so that he could come to Jesus. But, seeing how powerful the wind was, he became frightened, and as he started to sink he screamed, "Lord, save me!" And Jesus, quickly extending his hand, caught him and said to him, "You of little faith, why did you doubt?" And when they climbed*

into the boat, the wind stopped and suddenly the boat was at the shore toward which they were going. Those who were in the boat came to him and adored him saying, "Truly you are the son of God."

In this harmonized version the scene is set with brief but clear characteristics: it is evening, toward night at the start, but the incident occurs at the fourth watch between 3:00 A.M. and dawn. The disciples are laboring in the boat against a contrary wind. Jesus appears, walking on the water, but the disciples think they are seeing a *fantasma*. Reassured that it is Jesus, Peter attempts to walk toward him on the water and, because he is afraid and "of little faith," he begins to sink. Weak Christian faith buffeted by the strong winds of reality will not be sufficient; if Christ is not "in the boat," it will be a losing battle to bring Peter's bark to the shore toward which it is headed. This is neither obscure nor hidden. While Peter and Jesus are out on the water, however, Jesus instantly responds to Peter's human cry for help and extends his hand. He asks the question that contains the explanation as to why Peter was sinking: "Modice fidei, quare dubitaste?" They get back into the boat and, with Jesus now on board, the wind dies and suddenly their boat is at the shore they were seeking. The ending illuminates the origin of the faith problem and all who were in the boat adore Christ as the Son of God.

This perfect incident our author uses to illustrate the situation of the Saxons who had been baptized—placed in the boat—but who later had trouble believing the content of their new faith, that Jesus is the Son of God. The author's stratagem is to elaborate the scene in north Germanic terms and to increase the descriptive realism of the boat scene. One vital part, however, he chose to eliminate.

The Old High German translation of the scene (*Tatian* 81, 1–5; pp. 107–8) simply renders the first verses:

Abande giwortanemo eino was her that. Thaz
skef in mittemo sewe was giwuorphozit mit then
undon: was in widarwart wint. (81, 1)

It becoming evening, he [Jesus] was alone

there [on the mountain]. The boat in the middle
of the sea was being thrown [around] by the waves:
the wind was against them.

The *Heliand* completely alters the tone and once again emphasizes the location at the water's edge:

Tho te thes wateres stađe
samnodun thea gisiđos Cristes, the he imu habda selƀo
gicorane,
sie tueliƀi thurh iro trewa goda: ni was im tueho nigiean,
neƀu sie an that godes thionost gerno weldin
oƀar thene seo siđon. Tho letun sie suiđean strom,
hoh hurnidskip hluttron uđeon
skeđan skir water. Skred lioht dages
sunne warđ an sedle; the seoliđandean
naht neƀulo biwarp; nađidun erlos
forđwardes an flod; warđ thiu fiorđe tid
thera nehtes cuman–neriendo Crist
warode theo wagliđand–: tho ward wind mikil,
hoh weder afhaƀan: hlamodun uđeon,
strom an stamne; stridiun feridun
thea weros wiđer winde, was im wređ hugi
seƀo sorgono ful: selƀon ni wandun
laguliđandea an land cumen
thurh thes wederes gewin. (XXXV, 2902–16)

On the water's shore
gathered the disciples [gisiđos, followers, military
companions] of Christ,
whom He Himself had chosen
the twelve for their goodly faith; nor felt they doubt;
but in God's service they would gladly go
over the sea. They let the high-horned ship
cut through the strong stream, the clear wave and the
water sheer;
the light of day, the sun strode to rest. Night surrounded
the seafarers with mist; the earls strove on
forward in the flood. Now the fourth hour of

night was come. All-saving Christ
warded the wave-farers; the wind grew great,
the sea 'gainst the stem; with trouble they steered
the ship through [i.e., toward or against; wider] the
wind. The warriors grew fearful of mind,
their hearts filled with care. The lake-farers indeed
never believed that they would ever reach land
because of the battle [i.e., because of the gains of weather].
(Scott, pp. 99–100)

If the reader has the idea that the *Heliand* poet is portraying the disciples as nobles struggling in a Viking-style longboat to cross the Sea of Galilee, I would heartily agree.

We have already seen the boats described as "well-nailed." This is not a simple reference to sturdiness. For centuries northern boats had differed from Mediterranean ones in that they were lapstrake or clinker-built rather than carvel-built. This means that the outer planks were not nailed edge to edge, but overlapped each other slightly, much in the manner of siding on a house. Such a method requires less internal framing but mandates highly visible nailing of the strakes or planks. In addition our *non ignobilis vates* describes the apostolic boat as being "high-horned," indicating a northern type of craft called a double-ender in which both ends of the boat come to a point in plain view, much in the manner of a canoe. Mediterranean vessels were characterized by broad sterns. "High-horned" also calls to mind the graceful high stem and stern of a boat contemporary to the time of the *Heliand*, the Oseberg ship, which was found on a farm in Norway in 1904 and now rests in a museum in Oslo.[1] The phrase *skeđan skir water* or "cutting clear water" may also be an allusion to the effect of the *cutwater*—an extension of the stem on smaller vessels to allow better directional control. Landström mentions it in connection with eighth-century (northern) working vessels:

> The early Gotland pictorial stones—from the seventh and eighth centuries—already seem to show two different types of boat: those where the sterns form a sharp angle with the keel and those where the sterns curve gracefully up from the keel. It might have been thought that certain

> pictures were only badly drawn were it not for a carving found on the under side of a deck plank on the Oseberg ship which gives an almost naturalistic view of the bow of a vessel. And there we find almost the same broad cutwater that we have seen earlier in the Mediterranean.
>
> It is therefore believed that many vessels which sailed Scandinavian waters, especially the traders which were more dependent on good sailing ability than fighting craft, were equipped with such a cutwater.[2]

Whether or not the *Heliand* author is alluding specifically to a cutwater or to the sliding motion of the entire boat on calm seas, it seems he may well be giving his fellow missionaries to the Saxons, and perhaps even himself, an indirect compliment when he comments on Christ's faithful retinue "nor felt they doubt; / but in God's service they would gladly go / over the sea."

There is even more awareness of seafaring in the storm scene. With the coming of night, the fog and mist of the northern sea rolls in; there is no trace of clear Palestinian skies. The colder air of evening and the warm water produce *nebulo* 'fog'. When the wind gathers strength and the storm arises, our poet/missionary draws his own nautical conclusions from the Gospel phrase *erat enim contrarius ventus*, that is, the wind was against them. If the wind was so strong that the apostles were frightened, it would be wise to take the ship off course and either labor to keep the bow into the wind or, if the wind and waves were too strong, to turn and place the stern end to the wind and run before it. The author's simple phrase *strom an stamne*[3] eloquently describes the sailor's desperate attempts with shortened sail, oar, and steering board to keep the bow (or, if running, the stern) to the waves in order to avoid broaching (which would be to turn the low sides of a boat broadside to the waves, placing the craft in immediate danger of being swamped and sunk). The "high-horned stem," the author realizes only too well, must be kept to the waves.

The other fear of a sailor in a storm who is struggling to avoid being blown too much to leeward is also incorporated into the account. The apostle-sailors begin to fear that they will never reach land *'thurh thes wederes gewin'*, because of how much they are losing "to weather," that is, how much they are being forced downwind—slipping to leeward—because of the storm. This is an ocean seafarer's dread as well as that of a land-locked lake fisherman, if he is at all close to land. It is surprising how much traditional nautical knowledge and feelings are at the disposal of the *Heliand* poet. His gracious compliment to the retinue of Christ that they were such faithful vassals that they would not hesitate in God's service, but rather *gerno weldin/oƀar thene seo siđon* 'would gladly go over the sea' must have come easily to one whose predecessors on the German and Saxon mission had left their homes in the British Isles and had come over the sea.

The author's use of go *'siđ'* rather than sail *'ferian'* opens up another possibility of a more personal and spiritual hidden meaning in the passage. This phrase about the apostles going gladly over the sea initiates an entire pericope about Jesus "going on the sea." The author does not state, but perhaps implies, that the general going over the sea (to Germany and Saxony) was Christ himself going over the sea to the Saxons as he accompanied his men in the boat across the waters. As the poet states, *neriendo Crist warode thea wagliđand* "saving Christ protected the wave-riders [sailors]."[4]

The author has also pressed the incident into a clearer form than can be found in the Gospel. He has extended the length of the calm that occurs during the launching and initial sailing of the boat from its absence in the Gospel to seven lines describing the peaceful seashore with Christ, the *hluttron uđeon*, and *skir water*, the glassy waves and the clear water of perfect sailing conditions with a gentle, steady wind. He is thus able to tell the story as an *inclusio* or type of frame story with the structure *a, b, a*: calm, storm, calm. This simple structure not only is foreign to the Gospel pericope, but one is tempted to say it goes directly to the heart of the story and almost expresses its spiritual message in a clearer and more nautical form: calm, with Christ on the shore; storm, Christ absent, seems present only as specter; calm restored, with Christ present the boat is "ashore."

The effectiveness of the final calm is genuinely enhanced by the explicit description of a parallel calm in the beginning.[5] A worthwhile structural and instructional accommodation, definitely in the spirit of the evangelists.

In the midst of the sea, the retinue of Christ see him ***an themu see uppan selƀun gangan*** 'walking upon the sea' and their liege lord *'iro drohtin'*, who is also the holy king of heaven ***'helag hebencuning'***, tells them not to be afraid and promises real sailors' aid. In the Gospel the apostles are merely told not to be afraid. In the *Heliand*:

ik bium that barn godes,
is selƀes sunu, the iu wiđ thesemu see scal,
mundon wiđ thesan meristrom. (XXXV,2930–31)

I am the child of God,
His own son, who will help you with this sea,
with this ocean current.

Once again endearing Christ to the northern sailors, the author has him promise that he will be a help "to those in peril on the sea." The *Heliand* poet does this in such grand style that one is tempted to think he may also be fulfilling a religious need in the context of Saxon religion. Nordic sailors paid special reverence to Thor before undertaking a voyage, but I wonder if there was anything in the mythology of Thor (or Saxnot or Woden) that guarantees, as strikingly as the *Heliand*'s version of the walking on the water, that "the Child of God / His own Son" protects his own on the water.

To return to the story, Peter doubts and challenges the apparition.

Tho sprac imu en thero manno angegin
oƀar bord skipes, barwirđig gumo,
Petrus the godo–ni welde pine tholon,
wateres witi–: "ef thu it waldand sis", quađ he
herro the godo, so mi an minumu hugi thunkit,
het mi than tharod gangan te thi oƀar thesen geƀenes
 strom,
drokno oƀar diap water, ef thu min drohtin sis,
managoro mundboro. (XXXV,2931–37)

One of the men spoke back to him
overboard the ship, that worthy man,

Peter the good–he didn't want to suffer pain,
to feel the water's power–: "If you are the Almighty," he said,
"as I think inside you are, good Lord,
then tell me to come over to you across this seaway
dry across deep water, if you are my Chieftain,
Protector of many people."

The poet realizes the allusion in the Gospel to the Old Testament scene of the exodus where the Israelites went dry shod across the Red Sea and delicately explicates the allusion with the parenthetical phrase placed in the mouth of Peter, *drokno oƀar diap water* 'dry across deep water'. He even adapts it to this New Testament scene in which Christ is shown as being the same Lord of creation, able to rescue from the encroaching envelopment by the waters. Peter's question is also given a positive aspect in the second parenthesis in this section, *so mi an minumu hugi thunkit* 'as I think inside', lest the Saxon warrior be tempted to follow Peter's questioning and doubt also. Instead the reader is led into identification with Peter by sympathy with the nautical concreteness of Peter's shouting *oƀar bord*, by exclamations of his being worthy and good, and by Peter's admission of his human dread of suffering from feeling the water's power.

It should not be overlooked that the fear of the water at this point is a poetic expansion of the text. In the original there is no fear of the water mentioned. The disciples do not become frightened until they see the ghost walking toward them across the water, and it is only then that they cry out in fear *'pre timore clamaverunt'*. The unexpected appearance of Jesus is the first cause of the disciples' fear in the New Testament account, but the author of the *Heliand* has further expanded the cause to include the familiar fear of the water, the power of the sea, and thus brought the account into the range of well-known maritime experiences. When Christ tells Peter to come to him, Peter

stop af[6] themu stamme endi stridiun geng
forđ te is froian. (XXXV,2940–41)

stepped up on [or down from] the post[7] *and*

walked toward his lord.

Once again the *Heliand* legitimately expands the image in placing Peter in the end of the boat and describing the motion to get off the boat. When Peter, soon thereafter, begins to sink in the water as his doubts overwhelm him, he calls out to Christ for help and asks Christ not to desert his warrior knight (*thegan*/thane).

The *Heliand* depicts the next part of the story with great tenderness. The famous rebuke "O you of little faith" is completely eliminated and the rescue scene is made into a small frame story. In *Tatian* we have the following literal translation from the *Diatessaron*:

> Inti sliumo ther heilant thenenti sina hant
> fieng inan inti quad imo: luziles gilouben, bihiu
> zuehotus thu? Inti so sie tho gistigun in skef...
> (LXXXI,4)

> *And immediately the Savior put out his hand and caught*
> *him and said to him: "O you of little faith, why did you*
> *doubt?" And when they had climbed into the boat...*

The *Heliand* frames the scene by providing two separate times when Jesus reaches out to catch Peter. The first time he reaches out with extended arms and *antfeng ine mid is fađmun* 'caught him with his outstretched arms' (cf. Eng. *fathom*–the distance, six feet, between fully extended hands). Jesus then gives the inserted speech that is much milder than the original, telling Peter that he had to *getruoian wel* 'trust well' and to have *geloƀan te mi* 'faith in me', for then the sea would not have been able to impede his path. This instruction reemphasizes the importance of an *unwavering* faith in Christ, a point doubtless intended directly for the vacillating Saxons. Having said this, however, Jesus is then described as taking Peter *by the hand* and walking with him back to the boat:

> Tho nam ine alomahtig
> helag bi handen: tho warđ imu eft hlutter water
> fast under fotun, endi sie an fađi samad
> bedea gengun, antat sie oƀar bord skipes
> stopun fan themu strome, endi an themu stamne gesat

allaro barno bezt. (XXXV,2957–62]

The Almighty, the holy One, took him by
the hand: and immediately clear water became solid
under his feet, and they went together, both of them,
walking until they climbed on board the boat from
out of the sea, and then there sat by the stem post
the best of those who have ever been born.

We can see immediately that the *Heliand* author makes implicit imagery explicit by playing grace notes, as it were, as an enhancement of the original score. *Sie an fađi samad, beđea gengun* is not in the original, though it may be presumed. The author does not want it presumed; he wants it explicitly stated that Christ took Peter in his arms, that Peter needed trust and faith in Christ, and that Christ took Peter by the hand and they walked together back to the boat–and that it is Christ who sits in the bow of Peter's boat.

This amplification of the Gospel story conforms not only to the author's mission to instruct the wavering Saxons by bringing them into the story with Peter and with Christ, but it also conforms to the high veneration at the time for St. Peter. During this historic period, the pope referred to himself commonly, as we have said, not as the vicar of Christ but as the vicar of St. Peter, threatening even emperors that he would tell St. Peter if they did not behave as Christians and reminding them that, when they died, it would be Peter who would be standing before them with the keys to heaven in his hands. The emphasis, therefore, in the *Heliand* account of the story of the walking on the water is not so much that it was Christ who walked on the water as that—in this recounting—Christ *and* Peter walked on the water.

The *Heliand* author thus creates a clear and balanced form that shifts the emphasis from Christ's divine power and Peter's lack of faith to Christ's divine power and personal engagement for Peter and Peter's subsequent ability to walk on the water with Christ.

The structure of this pericope might be diagramed as follows:

Calm — departure from the shore

Storm —
- a Peter alone: sinks
- b Peter *and* Christ
- a *Peter with Christ: walks*

Calm — arrival at destination

Where the *Heliand* author has elaborated an implicit section or filled in a pause, I have placed italics. From this it is easy to see that the *Diatessaron* Gospel is being given a 3 x 3 or a triple inclusion form in order to focus on Peter's need to be taken by the hand of Christ in order to maintain his Christian belief. This is a spiritual and pastoral religious meditation in poetic form. The author has a keen sense of balanced and recitable language, much in the manner of the ancient Iliad, as well as the Germanic epics. He strives, through the embracing form of poetic images, not to rebuke the Saxon fishermen for having little faith, but to reassure them that the Almighty, the Holy One, is waiting with outstretched arms to take them by the hand across the perilous water, back to the safety of Peter's boat. And, in the boat, it is Christ himself, not Charlemagne, who is seated in the bow.

Notes

1. Cf. Bjorn Landström, *The Ship, An Illustrated History*, (Garden City: Doubleday, 1967), pp. 58–59.

2. Ibid., p. 57. All the above are extremely well illustrated in Landström's book.

3. A variant (*M*) has "storm" for "strom," which may or may not simply be a felicitous metathesis.

4. It could also be argued that the *s* of *siđon* is necessary for the line's alliteration. It may indeed be true that the *s* increases the alliterative quality of the line but it is not entirely necessary since the line already contains the expected three accented sibilants: *ođar thane seo siđon. / Tho letun sie suiđean strom*. Descendants of the New Critics will appreciate the sound of the wind in line 2916, as the apostles struggle for control of the boat: "thea *w*eros *w*iđer *w*inde, *w*as im *w*ređ hugi" [The men against the wind were in a terrified mood].

5. The Gospel account simply begins *"in medias res: Vespere autem facto, solus erat ibi. Navicula autem in medio mari iactabatur fluctibus"* [When evening came he was alone there. The boat however in the middle of the sea was being tossed about by the waves].

6. *C* has *fan* 'from' and I prefer it for the sake of the sense with stem or stern post.

7. Or possibly stem post; though we are uncertain which it is, the stern (or stem) is more particular and concrete than the original in that the term locates Peter in the ends of the boat. The Gospels give Peter no particular location in the boat: *Diatessaron*: *descendens Petrus de navicula*; Old High German *Tatian*: *nidarstiganter Petrus fon themo skefe*.

5

THE LORD OF THE RUNES

> VII. Si quis corpus defuncti hominis secundum ritum paganorum flamma consumi fecerit et ossa eius ad cinerem redierit, capitae punietur.
>
> *If anyone should cause the body of a dead man to be consumed by flame and his bones reduced to ashes in accordance with pagan ritual, let him suffer capital punishment. (Capitulatio de partibus Saxoniae, p. 38)*

Woden and Thor are nowhere explicitly cited in the *Heliand*, yet they are present. The author did not quail before incorporating expressive imagery of more ultimate divine forces—*wurd* and *metod*—into the Gospel; nevertheless he seems to have felt a pastoral need to handle Woden and Thor more carefully. This is probably due to the fact that, although *wurd* and *metod* were the most feared forces in Germanic religion and were acknowledged to determine the time of *ragnarok/domsdag/mutspelli* 'the last day', these ultimate entities were not popularly worshiped or prayed to since they could not be moved. Prayer and sacrifice traditionally have had not only adoration as their end, but also the persuasion of moveable objects for healing, safety on the sea, rescue from enemies, fertility, and so forth, as can be seen in early fragments such as the *Merseburger Zaubersprüche*.[1]

Fate and time seem to have been conceived in such implacable and utterly neutral terms as to be totally beyond the reach of religion; when Fate begins to draw near, even in the *Heliand*, unless Christ is there, one's doom is sealed. Woden and Thor, however, are conceived in much more human terms. They can be persuaded by religious practice to stop causing storms, for example, as perhaps seen in Thor's hammer neck medallions found in Viking seafarers' graves.

The *Heliand* author must show Christ to be similar in appeal to Wise Woden and Mighty Thor, but he must also be shown to be of higher divine stature than either of them and he must be able to change Fate's merciless decisions rather than being subject to them. In Germanic mythology, Woden the Wise will be devoured at the "twilight of the gods" while struggling with Fenrir—the great wolf whose cavernous mouth is the emptiness of the abyss. Thor will be killed by the poison of the great world serpent, who is associated with the outermost circle of the ocean and whose coils represent the edge of the universe. The analagous Gospel incidents by which the *Heliand* ingeniously selects and interprets to show Christ's superiority to both the wolf and the serpent are the resurrection and the walking on the water. If Christ can survive the jaws of the wolf and bend the will of Fate, if he can give secret wisdom to men, he is a new and infinitely more powerful Woden, a new Lord of the Runes.

Magnus Magnusson comments on the meaning of this title and translates the famous passage from the *Havamal*.

> [Odin] is also credited with the discovery of runes, the semi-magical system of writing incised on bone, wood or stone by the Norsemen before the introduction of the Roman alphabet... Runes were mostly used for memorial inscriptions, but they were also used for secret charms or curses. Their magical association goes all the way back to an enigmatic myth about their discovery by Odin after he had ritually hanged and stabbed himself:
>
> I know that I hung

on the windswept tree
for nine whole nights
pierced by the spear
and given to Odin—
Myself to myself
On that tree
Whose roots
No one knows.

They gave me not bread
Nor drink from the horn;
Into the depths I peered,
I grasped the runes,
Savouring I grasped them,
And fell back.[2]

This passage, with its allusions to the darker side of Odin worship such as sacrificing enemies hung in sacred trees and possible Byzantine Christian influence "myself to myself"; "pierced by the spear" concludes with an unmistakably Germanic passage: the god of consciousness is risking an approach to death, hanging on the cosmic tree of life and piercing himself with a spear to gain the hidden power of knowledge. He sees the depths open, reaches down and seizes the knowledge hidden there—the runes—and screams. This is a pointed and terrifying contrast to the God who reveals himself to Moses in the burning bush, as well as on the Sermon on the Mount and the transfiguration on Mount Tabor. The *Heliand* author begins the northern Germanic transformation of Christ as he who knows the secret runes (and teaches them to his disciples) with the first major scene in the public life of Christ the teacher—the Baptism in the Jordan.

At the end of song eleven, the *Heliand* adds a phrase to the Baptist's teaching that marks it unmistakably: *Ne latad ewan hugi twiflien!* (XI,948) 'Do not let your minds doubt!'

Jesus' baptism is then clearly placed in the context of a mass baptism. The author is well aware of the memory of many Saxons who had been baptized with Frankish spears at their backs. To sharpen the image, the author alters the motivation for receiving John's baptism from one of *repentance* for one's sins to a conversion into a new *faith*. The people along the Jordan are thus described as coming to baptism *endi iro gilobon antfengun* (XI,953) 'and received their faith'. The *Heliand*'s hearers are led to feel that the baptism of Jesus took place in their own baptismal context of a few years before; namely, that of being given a new faith rather than that of repentance for sins. To insure that this slight change of emphasis will transform the context, the author leaves nothing to chance, but stresses the image of mass baptism two more times in lines 965–67 and 977, before Christ comes up from the water:

> thar Iohannes an Iordana strome
> allan langan dag liudi manage
> dopte diurlico.
>
> *There was John on Jordan's stream*
> *all day long—many people he*
> *was baptizing dearly.*
>
> Iohannes stod,
> dopte allan dag druhtfolc mikil
> werod an watere endi ok waldand Krist
> heran heƀencuning handun sinun
> an allaro badҨo them beston.
>
> *John stood there*
> *every day baptizing the great mass of people,*
> *people in the water, including the almighty Christ,*
> *the lordly king of heaven, with his [John's] own hands,*
> *in the best of all baths.*

The poetic implication that Jesus had been one of the Saxons as they were crowded into the water by the Franks is gently and beautifully done by a triple repetition of what in Luke 3:11 is only an ablative absolute in a subordinate clause: *"cum baptizaretur omnis populus et Ihesu baptizato et orante* / tho gitoufit was al thaz folc inti themo heilante gitoufitemo into betontemo" (*Tatian* XIV,3) [when all the people were being baptized, and Jesus (the Savior), baptized and praying]. One might suppose that the author, meditating on this scene, saw the small phrase *omnis populus / al thaz folc* and felt it suggested his own people.

It is only as Christ comes up out of the water, with all the people, that it becomes clear who he is. In the New Testament accounts it is revealed from heaven that he is God's Son: the heavens open, a voice from above says, "You are my beloved Son in whom I am well pleased," and the Spirit of God in the form of a dove—as predicted to John—comes down upon him. In *Tatian*'s harmony (XIV,4–7), the following phrases are used for the descent of the Holy Spirit and its resting upon Christ: *venientem super se* / quementan ubar sih 'coming upon him', and *"vidi spiritum descendentem quasi columbam de caelo, et mansit super eum* / ih gisah geist nidarstigantan samaso tubun fon himile, into woneta ubar inan" [I saw the spirit coming down like a dove from heaven and it remained over him].

The author makes a small change:

So he tho that land ofstop
so anthlidun tho himiles doru, endi quam the helago gest
fon them alowaldon ƀane te Kriste:
—was im an gilicnissie lungres fugles,
diurlicara duƀun—endi sat im uppan uses drohtines ahslu,
wonoda im oƀar them waldandes barne. (XII,984–89)

And as he stepped up onto the land
the doors of heaven opened and there came the Holy Spirit
from the Almighty above, to Christ:
—it was like a powerful bird
a magnificent dove—and it sat upon our Lord's shoulder,
remaining over the Ruler's Son.

The original text makes no attempt to specify any particular place above (much less *on*) the Savior where the dove came to rest. The author specifies: *endi sat im uppan uses drohtines ahslu* 'and it sat upon our Lord's shoulder'. I am sure my readers are familiar with the iconography of Woden/Odin and have already sped ahead to my conclusion. Woden is always depicted with the black ravens Nunin and Hugin (memory and mind) perched squarely on his shoulders. They whisper into his ear and keep him aware of all things. In placing the powerful white dove not just above Christ, but right on his shoulder, the *Heliand* author has portrayed Christ, not only as the Son of the All-Ruler, but also as a new Woden. This deliberate image of Christ triumphantly astride the land with the magnificent bird on his shoulders (the author is perhaps a bit embarrassed that the bird is an unwarlike dove!) is an image intended to calm the fears and longings of those who mourn the loss of Woden and who want to return to the old religion's symbols and ways. With this image, Christ becomes a Germanic god, one into whose ears the Spirit of the Almighty whispers.

Should anyone object that this image is pagan and unorthodox, the author carefully adds a line after specifying *the shoulder* reasserting the vague *oƀar* 'above' of the synoptic tradition. It is clear that the *Heliand* monk intended that the image of Christ supersede that of Woden. This vivid picture of Christ with the dove on his shoulder offers both a comforting similarity to the old high god and a reassuring difference as well. The *Heliand* suggests that when the Saxons were being baptized by force in the River Lippe, the twilight of the old gods had come; but now that the almighty God stood among the people—a recognizable figure—with the familiar divine bird on his shoulders, they had not been abandoned.

This powerful Germanic-Christian poetic synthesis of the *Heliand* may well have been carried far into the Nordic Viking world. Magnusson describes the famous Ragnarok Stone (c. 950 A.D.) at Kirk Andreas on the Isle of Man:

> Another [Manx Stone], in Kirk Andreas, depicts Odin the All-Father, naked and with a raven on his shoulder, gripped in the jaws of the ferocious wolf Fenrir which was destined to kill him in the Norse version of Armageddon, the Ragnarok (Doom of the Gods). The reverse shows a belted figure bearing aloft the Cross and the Book, trampling on a serpent... The juxtaposition of the two scenes represents most effectively the concept of Christ reigning in Odin's stead.[3]

In addition, one might add that the devouring of Odin takes place under a large Celtic cross, perhaps implying that the coming of (Celtic) Christianity is itself the Ragnarok, the twilight of the gods. There has been speculation that the *Heliand*'s unique synthesis might have had little influence on the conversion of the north. This stone, however, so far from Saxony, would appear to give highly credible evidence to the contrary.

The people who came in vast numbers to baptism came also to be taught, *liudi te lerun* (XII,953). If Christ is God's Son and supersedes Woden, he should know and teach the secret runes of existence, as had Woden. It is perhaps for this reason that Christ is depicted similarly to Woden as a knower of secret wisdom, and also that the Sermon on the Mount occupies such a disproportionately large amount of the *Heliand*. Fully eight of the seventy-two songs are devoted to it. In recounting the story, Christ is described as revealing to his followers, who are gathered in a circle around him, the divine spell and the secret runes by which one can come into contact with God and reach heaven.

The author sets the scene simply. Christ is on a mountain *'an enna berg uppan'*, calling the Twelve to him as in *Tatian*'s Harmony, but with a slight change of emphasis. The *Heliand* account repeats that Christ was up on a mountain (XV,1249 and 1270), as if to emphasize his separation and elevation from common mortals. In calling the Twelve to come to him, it is visually clear that they are being raised to the royal retinue and thereby ennobled. The tenth one is told to go *mid them gisiđun* (XV,1269) 'with the retinue', and Bartholomew is to come up out of the mountain and separate himself from the other *folke* (XV,1271), clearly an appeal to the social class consciousness of the warrior nobility living in their hill fortresses. More than that, however, they are being called by Christ *te theru runu* (XV,1273) 'to a secret council':

> Tho umbi thana neriendon Krist nahor gengun sulike gesidos, so he im selbo gecos, waldand undar them werode. (XVI,1278–81)
>
> *Then around the saving Christ there approached those companions whom he chose for himself as he went ruling among the people.*

Having culturally transformed the scene by changing it from a rabbinic to a runic (i.e., secret warriors') council with the wise leader, the *Heliand* also alters the geography to that of the North Sea coast. With an incredible economy of expression and image, he transforms the well-known "you are the salt of the earth, but if salt has lost its taste how shall its saltiness be restored? What is it good for but to be thrown out and trampled under foot by men?" (Matt. 5:13) into the following:

than is im so them salte, the man bi sees stađe
wido tewirpit: than it te wihti ni dog,
ac it firiho barn fotun spurnat
gumon an greote (XVI,1370–73)

[If you turn away from this teaching] then ye are like
unto the salt which is scattered
wide on the seashore; then it has worth to none,
and the bairns of the land-folk will walk in it with their feet,
men grind it into grit ["grit" meaning the beach sand]
(Scott, pp. 45–46)

Even the biblical warning that not to carry out the words of Christ is like "a foolish man who built his house on sand"[4] is seized upon immediately as a chance to change the scene to the seashore:

So duot eft manno so huilic, so thesun minun ni wili
lerun horien ne thero lestien wiht,
so duot the unwison erla gelico
ungewittigon were, the im be wateres stađe
an sande wili selihus wirkean,
thar it westrani wind endi wago strom,
sees uđeon teslaad; ne mag im sand endi greot
gewređien wiđ themu winde, ac wirđit teworpan than,
tefallen an themu flode, huand it an fastoro nis
erđu getimbrod. (XXI,1815–1824)

Scott translates:

Thus doeth each man, who willeth not
to hear these my teachings, or to carry them out:
He acteth indeed like the unwise earl,
like the witless world man, who on the water's shore,
on the sand itself, would set up his great-halled house,
where the western wind and the waves of the stream,

the tides of the sea do tear it, sand and grit cannot
hold it up 'gainst the flood, since it stood not fast,
firmly timbered in earth. (pp. 61–62)

The poet is taking such great pains to saxonize the Sermon on the Mount that we can assume he was quite aware of the difficulty of persuading the Saxon warrior nobles to accept some of the most basic tenets contained in it: blessed are the meek, turn the other cheek, love your enemies. To his credit, he does not shirk from the battle with this problem, but faces it head on, sometimes even intensifying the sermon's moral teachings on war and vengeance by using very local and unmistakable language. Structurally he keeps to the form of the sermon in the Gospel harmony, which has the Lord's Prayer in the center and the teachings loosely framing it on both sides—as in Matthew—a structure he doubtless found familiar and useful.

The first of the Beatitudes (Matt: 5), which Christ reveals to his circle of twelve noble warriors, "Blessed are the poor in spirit for theirs is the kingdom of heaven" [*beati pauperes spiritu, quoniam ipsorum est regnum caelorum* / salige sint thie thar arme sind in geiste, wanta thero ist gottes rihhi (*Tatian* 22,7)] becomes in the *Heliand*:

quađ that thie salige warin,
man an thesaro middilgardun, thie her an iro mode warin
arme thurh odmodi: "them is that ewana riki
suiđo helaglic an heƀanwange
sinlif fargeƀen." (XVI,1300–4)

He said those were blessed,
of the people in this middle realm, who, in their attitude,
were poor through humility: "for to them is granted
the eternal kingdom in all holiness,
eternal life on the meadows of heaven."

Humility is not seen as a manly virtue in Germanic tradition, as can be seen, for example, in *Beowulf*. Seeking fame on earth is virtuous instead. To make the new teaching more palatable, the author has placed the first part of this Beatitude in the less obtrusive mode of indirect discourse and the second part, which promises eternal bliss, he cites directly from the Savior's own mouth. Moreover he uses ***an iro "mode"; thurh od-modi*** as though to suggest that this statement might also be justifiable ***precisely*** because of the verbal similarity of the words for attitude and humility. Having planted this seed, he quickly elaborates on how blissful the meadows of heaven will be. Unlike *Tatian* he clearly interprets, however inconvenient it may be, what "poor in spirit" means.

The second Beatitude, "blessed are the meek, for they will possess the earth" [*beati mites, quoniam ipsi possidebunt terram* / salige sint mandware, wanta thie bisizzent erda (*Tatian* XXII,9)] must also have clashed with the Saxon warriors' concept of virtue. The author translates tactfully:

> Quađ that oc salige warin
> mađmundie man: "thie motun thie marion erđe,
> ofsittien that selƀe riki." (XVI,1304–6)

> *He said that those too were blessed*
> *who were gentle people: "they will be allowed to possess the great earth,*
> *the same kingdom."*

"Blessed are those who mourn, for they will be consoled" [*beati qui lugent, quoniam ipsi consolabuntur* / salige sint thie thar wuofent, wanta thie werdent gifluobrit (*Tatian* XXII,101)] receives an unusually religious interpretation perhaps due to the commentaries:

> Quađ that oc salige warin
> thie hir wiopin iro wammun dadi; "thie motun eft willion gebidan,
> frofre an iro frahon rikia." (XVI,1306–8)

> *He said that those also were blessed,*
> *who have wept over their evil deeds; "they will receive according to their desire,*
> *consolation in their lord's kingdom."*

There is no doubt a pastoral motive behind using such a spiritualizing interpretation. It may be that his constant appeal to the vacillating Saxons to "believe and not to doubt" may be joined with the author's consoling appeal to repent the evil deeds of the past. The author tends to be specific in his interpretations and this is clear in the fourth Beatitude.

"Blessed are those who hunger and thirst for justice, for they shall be satisfied" [*beati qui esuriunt et sitiunt justitiam, quoniam ipsi saturabuntur* / salige sint thie thar hungerent inti thurstent reht, wanta thie werdent gisatote. (XXII,11)]. The *Tatian* here is so literal as to be uncomfortably strained "to hunger and thirst justice." The *Heliand* has no such problem and the author begins with no resort to indirect discourse.

> Salige sint oc, the sie hir frumono gilustid,
> rincos, that sie rehto adomien. Thes motun sie werdan an them rikia drohtines
> gifullit thurh iro ferhton dadi: sulicoro motun sie frumono bicnegan,
> thie rincos, thie hir rehto adomiad, ne williad an runun beswican
> man, thar sie at mahle sittiad. [XVI,1308–12]

> *Blessed also are those who desired to do good,*
> *men who judged fairly, this is what they themselves*
> *will be satisfied with in the Lord's kingdom because of*
> *their good deeds: they will reach such favor,*
> *these men who judged fairly, that they will not be deceived by secrets*
> *as they sit there at the banquet.*

This Beatitude represents a clear change from a passive interpretation to an active one. The author has transposed the imagined subject of the Beatitude from that of a peasant or serf desiring that justice *be done* to him, to a member of the nobility. The *Heliand* thus uses this Beatitude to praise those Saxon nobles who attempt to *administer* justice fairly to those under them and implicitly condemns those who do not. To the counter argument that those who try to *do good* and give fair judgments are frequently deceived, he replies that they will not be deceived when they are seated at the Lord's banquet in heaven—a beautiful expansion and interpretation of "they will be satisfied." The author has a penchant for active interpretations. In this context it is curious to recall Goethe's *Faust*, where "in the beginning was the word" is interpreted as "in the beginning was the deed" (Faust I,1224–37)]. In the *Heliand*, however, this active interpretation reveals the social class being addressed.

In the fifth Beatitude, "blessed are the merciful, for they shall be shown mercy" [*beati misericordes, quoniam ipsi misericordiam consequentur / salige sint thie thar sint miltherze, wanta sie folgent miltidun* (XXII,12)], *Tatian*, in the Old High German, may even have invented a word in order to translate each syllable into German—*miseri-cors; milt-herze*. The *Heliand* merely adjusts the phrasing slightly so as to suggest the generous ring-giver, the kind and generous depiction of noble warrior kings in the tradition as we know it from *Beowulf*:

Salige sind oc them hir mildi wirđit
hugi an heliđo briostun: them wirđit the helago drohtin,
mildi mahtig selƀo. (XVI,1312–15)

Blessed are those who have kind
and generous feelings within a hero's chest: the powerful holy Lord
will be kind and generous to them.

The author's worry, once again, that some of these Beatitudes might strike his audience as designed for someone less than a warrior shows through. He remains faithful to the text, but adroitly transposes the person addressed, as he did in the fourth Beatitude. While it may not be appealing to think of a paid north Germanic *warrior* as mild (i.e., kind and generous), nevertheless it is a common and respected term for the *lord* of those warriors to be perceived as powerful, but *mild*. Conforming with and appealing to that heroic tradition, the author has justified what is otherwise a somewhat embarrassing statement in the warrior tradition. Once again the author skillfully places an obligation on the lords of the clans and tribes to act with kindness, if they expect their Lord to be generous and kind with them. The *Heliand* author is forming a new Germanic-Christian synthesis of the ideal man: a composite of personal strength and interior gentleness, a "heroic chest with a kind heart inside." This idea persisted well into the Middle Ages and, in many transformations, is obviously still to be found today.

"Blessed are the clean of heart, for they will see God" [*beati mundo corde, quoniam ipsi deum videbunt / salige sint thie thar sint subere in herzon, wanta thie gisehent got* (XXII,13)] does not merit too much expansion by our author. Though important to Matthew's Gospel because of the controversy between Jesus and the Pharisees over interior versus exterior purification and cleanliness, it is perhaps too rooted in its original Jewish context to be of major interest for a Saxon audience. Still the *Heliand* author alters it, changing it from a passive description of a state of being "blessed *are* the clean of heart" to a beatification of *acting* to achieve the state "have cleaned":

> Salige sind oc undar thesaro managon thiodu,
> thie hebbiad iro herta gehrenod: thie motun thane hebenbes waldand
> sehan an sinum rikea. (XVI,1314–15)

> *Blessed also are those among these people who have cleaned their heart: they will see the ruler of heaven in his kingdom.*

The seventh Beatitude must have sorely tempted the author to evade its implications. Surely no instruction could be quite as difficult for a proud warrior society to accept as "blessed are the peacemakers, for they will be called the sons of God" [*beati pacifici, quoniam filii dei vocabuntur / salige sint thie thar sint sibbisame, wanta sie gotes barn sint sinemnit* (XXII,9)]. The *Heliand* author does not sidestep the teaching, but prudently finds common ground. It may be a point of manly honor to fight when challenged, but no warrior code approves of the person who precipitates conflict or who continually causes himself and others to appear in the lord's court. Thus the *Heliand* author interprets:

> Quađ that oc salige warin,
> thie the friđusama undar thesemu folke libbiod endi ni williad eniga fehta gewirken
> saca mid iro selboro dadiun: thie motun wesan suni drohtines genemnide,

hwande he im wil genadig werđen; thes motun sie niotan lango
selƀon thes sines rikies. (XVI,1316–20)

He also said those people were blessed
who live in peace among their people and who do not want to start any fights,
or court cases, by their own deeds: they will be called the sons of the Lord
for he will be gracious to them; they will long enjoy his kingdom.

There is also a more subtle change in the second part. Having appealed to a warrior's dislike of people who start fights and have to appear in court, he manages further to justify this Beatitude on the grounds that God is not just the heavenly God, he is also the Lord—and a lord has responsibility (as even a warrior knight would gladly admit) for the peaceful order of his kingdom. Where *Tatian* says that the peacemakers will be called the sons of God *'filii dei / gotes barn'*, the Heliand says that peacemakers will be called sons of the Lord *'suni drohtines'*. He expands the point in court language to explain that that is why he will be gracious to them, the implication being that, as the clan-lord's sons, they share responsibility for the tranquility of the lord's territory.

In the eighth Beatitude there is a return to the psychological and political state of the Saxons after their subjection by the Franks. *Tatian* says, *"Beati qui persecutionem patiuntur propter justitiam, quoniam ipsorum est regnum caelorum / salige sint thie thar ahtnessi sint tholenti thuruh reht, wanta iro ist himilo rihhi"* (XXII,15) [blessed are those who suffer persecution for justice' sake, for theirs is the kingdom of heaven]. The *Heliand* author, however, finds that even here Christ has had something to say to the Saxons. The author's explicitly political interpretation of the eighth Beatitude expresses his deep sympathy for the subjected state of his people under the rule of their more powerful, older Christian neighbors:

Quađ that oc salige warin

thie rincos, the rehto weldin, endi thurh that tholod
rikioro manno
heti endi harmquidi: them is oc an himile eft
godes wang forgeben endi gestlic lif
aftar te ewandage, so is io endi ni cumit
welan wunsames. (XVI,1320-25)

He said also that blessed were
the men who want justice; and who because of that suffer
more powerful lords'
hatred and verbal abuse: to them is granted in heaven
God's meadow and spiritual life
afterwards for eternal days, thus the end will never come
of beatific happiness!

The central point of the Sermon on the Mount, however, is not the eight Beatitudes, which are placed at the beginning, but rather the Lord's Prayer, which holds the middle position in the Sermon. If one concedes that the purpose of religion is to attain access to God, the Beatitudes can be said to be a Christian promise of eventual access. The magic runes, however, gave immediate, here-and-now access to the Germanic gods. The Beatitudes were God's spell, but the author must also satisfy a need for an equivalent to magic runic sayings or teachings for healing, such as:

ben zi bene
glid zi glide
sose gelimedet sin.

Bone to bone
limb to limb
as if they were glued.[5]

Having already presented the image of Christ as a Woden figure with the dove on his shoulder, the author—with a magical genius of his own—quietly presents the Lord's Prayer as the secret runes Christ conveys to his followers.

This literary conveying of the Our Father as runic is not, of course, taken up by the *Tatian*, which faithfully translates the Latin, *Domine, doce nos orare sicut Iohannes docuit discipulos suos,* with Drohtin, *leri unsih beton, soso Iohannes lerta sine iungiron* 'Lord, teach us to pray just as John taught his disciples' (XXXIV,5). The *Heliand* also has the disciples request Christ to teach them to pray as John does *'so Iohannes duot'*, and how they should greet the ruling God *'hwo sie waldand sculun, / godan grotean'* (XIX,1591–94). The disciples culminate their request with: *gerihti us that geruni* (XIX,1595) 'Teach us the secret runes'. Scott renders this passage beautifully, keeping the alliteration and managing to fully convey the sense of Germanic religion by changing the verb: "Reveal thou the runes" (p. 54). The Lord's Prayer thus becomes most specifically the replacement for Woden's runic charms that were relied on in the north to give access to the divine. Jesus is depicted, as Woden, knowing secret sayings that grant divine contact and placing power into the hands of selected followers who know the secret formulas. Now this information is revealed and given to the Saxons! Although this can be construed as a somewhat inflated context for the humble and simple words of the Lord's Prayer, it is not much different from the treatment given it by Matthew, who also treated it as a secret revealed, as the central part of the new Torah given by the new Moses to the new Israel on the mountain.

The *Heliand* also skillfully interprets the Our Father as a prayer that calls for action on the part of the person praying:

Fadar usa firiho barno
thu bist an them hohon himila rikea,
gewihid si thin namo wordo gehwilico.
Cuma thin craftag riki.
Werđa thin willeo oƀar thesa werold alla
so sama an erđo, so thar uppa ist
an them hohon himilo rikea,
Gef us dago gehwilikes rad, drohtin the godo,
thina helaga helpa, endi alat us, heƀenes ward,
managoro mensculdio, al so we ođrum mannum doan,
Ne lat us farledean leđa wihti
so forđ an iro willeon, so wi wirđige sind,
ac help us wiđar allun ubilon dadiun. (XIX,1600-12)

Father of us, the sons of men,

You are in the high heavenly kingdom,
blessed be your name in every word.
May your mighty kingdom come.
May your will be done over all this world—
just the same on earth as it is up there
in the high heavenly kingdom.
Give us support each day, good Lord,
Your holy help; and pardon us, protector of heaven,
our many crimes, just as we do to other human beings.
Do not let evil creatures lead us off
to do their will, as we deserve,
but help us against all evil deeds.[6]

Even the simple injunction, "hallowed be thy name," is turned into an implicitly more concrete call to action: not just may God's name be hallowed, but may it be hallowed in every word spoken. He who is addressed as the protector of heaven, a title that seems at once not only to allude to, but to imply supersedence of the warder of heaven—Woden—is asked, not for daily bread, but for daily support. As Father and source of the runes and of wisdom, he is not asked to "give us this day our daily bread" but our daily *support* of advice and help, *'rad'* and *'helpa'*. It may be that the author's listeners would have thought it lazy to ask heaven for bread, so the expression was broadened to include more practical support, the support of a lord.

Furthermore, the *Heliand* poet treats the supplication, "lead us not into temptation," in a very ingenious way. It is difficult to imagine God deliberately leading us into tempting situations, as the original prayer may be interpreted. The *Heliand* monk solves this somewhat puzzling phrase by attributing our circumstances of temptation to evil creatures. In every mythology there are variants of gnomes and trolls and "little people" who can be blamed for things that go wrong. The author skillfully takes advantage of this, but not in such a way as to let his human listeners feel blameless, for he inserts "as we deserve" after he has asked that the evil creatures be not allowed to "lead us off to do their will." He even refuses to let evil be objectified in the last petition, as if we are asking to be delivered from an evil that is an outsider attacking us.

He pointedly makes the last petition a plea for help against the actions we perform ourselves: ***help us widar allun ubilon dadiun.***

Having heard the holy spell and been told the secret runes, the disciples are sent off to those wise enough to see in this a treasure to be guarded as carefully as did Beowulf's deadly, final antagonist. The warning not to find fault with others lest, in searching for the speck in another's eye, one fails to notice the beam in one's own, is written in terms that evoke once again the felling of trees:

te hwi scalt thu enigan man besprekan
brođar thinan, that thu undar is brahon gesehas
halm an is ogon, endi gehuggean ni willi
thana suaran balcon, the thu an thinoro siuni hađbas,
hard trio endi hebig. Lat thi that an thinan hugi
fallan. (XX,1703–7)

How will you reprove anyone,
your brother, that under his eyebrows you see
a splinter in his eye, when you wish to know nothing of
the heavy beam that you have in your own eye—
a hard tree and heavy. *See that the tree of your attitude*
falls.

Here may be much of our author's spiritual transformation of the frightful manner of the conversion of the Saxons. In a way we might consider the passage addressed to Frankish and Anglo-Saxon missionaries—to Boniface and even to Charlemagne. It is also addressed more widely. No Saxon, hearing this, could help but feel he was being called to fell the tree of criticism of others and to advance beyond resentment.

The second allusion in this passage—the felling of revered order—clearly speaks the mind of the *Heliand* poet. In the Sermon on the Mount, Jesus is portrayed by Matthew to be taking great pains to reassure that he has not come to destroy the law and the prophets, but to fulfill them; ***non veni solvere, sed adimplere / ni quam ih zi losenne, uzouh zi fullenne*** (*Tatian* 25,4). In the *Heliand* this is translated:

Ni wanniat gi thes mit wihtiu, that ic bi thiu an thesa
werold quami,

that ic thana aldan eu irrien willie
fellean undar thesemu folke. (XVII,1420–22)

Do not think at all that I have come into this world
because I wanted to destroy the old law,
to chop it down amongst this people.

The *Heliand* monk's effort to keep the good that he sees in the old Germanic heroic poetic tradition may well be what he sees here as the old law, *'thana aldan eu'*, and sympathizes with Christ's effort to proclaim a new religion's law without destroying the old. This is seen in the *Heliand*'s exposition of the wisdom of the teachers of the Magi in the East. Christ also has a divine bird above his shoulder and, consequently, he may not have approved of the ruthless destruction of the tree of Woden. To emphasize this point, the *Heliand* monk repeats the same sentiment within six lines, inserting the verb *fell*:

Ni quam ic an thesa werold te thiu,
that ic *feldi* thero forasagono word. (XVII,1428–29)

I did not come into this world
to chop down the word of the prophets.

The reproof of the Franks is perhaps negative, but gives a deeper look into the author's mind and his intention of putting the Good News into the form of a spell, a god's spell: to sing the song of the Savior to the melodies and refrains of the old music—that Christ might live in the hearts of his Nordic countrymen as a compatriot and that Woden, and the unfortunate past, might now be able to sleep in peace.

Notes

1. Wilhelm Braune. *Althochdeutsches Lesebuch* (Tübingen: Max Niemeyer Verlag, 1958), p. 86.

2. Magnus Magnusson. *The Vikings* (New York: Elsevier-Dutton, 1980), pp. 11-12.

3. Ibid., pp. 173–74. Illustration of the stone, p. 173.

4. Matt. 7:26–27. "And everyone who hears these words of mine and does not do them will be like a foolish man who built his house upon the sand; and the rain fell and the floods came, and the winds blew and beat against that house, and it fell."

5. *Merseburger Zaubersprüche* in Braune, *Lesebuch*, p. 86.

6. For contrast, the literal Our Father in *Tatian* is quite similar to the new High German version:

Fater unser/Vater unser,
thu thar bist in himile, /der Du bist in Himmel,
si giheilagot thin name/geheiligt werde Dein Name,
queme thin rihhi, /zu uns komme Dein Reich,
si thin willo, /Dein Wille geschehe,
so her in himile ist, so si her in erdu/wie im Himmel,
also auch auf Erden.
unsar brot tagalihhaz gib uns hiutu, /Unser tägliches
Brot gib uns heute,
inti furlaz uns unsara sculdi/und vergib uns unsere
Schuld,
so wir furlazemes unsaren sculdigon, /wie auch wir ver-
geben unsern Schuldigern,
inti ni gileitest unsih in costunga, /und führe uns nicht
in Versuchung,
uzouh arlosi unseh fon ubile. (34,6) /sondern erlöse uns
von dem Übel.

6
THE FINAL BATTLE: *CAPTIVAM DUXIT CAPTIVATATEM*

XXII. Iubemus ut corpora christianorum Saxanorum ad cimiteria ecclesiae deferantur et non ad tumulus paganorum.

We do command that the bodies of Christian Saxons are to be brought to the cemeteries of the church and not to the mound-graves of the pagans. **(*Capitulatio de partibus Saxoniae*, p. 41)**

To interpret the passion and death of Christ, the author abandons allusions to Woden and Thor, although the myth of the final battle of the gods—and their defeat—would have made such a projection possible. He also ceases the references to the North Sea and the longboats. Instead he returns to the old epic stories of the warrior culture and depicts Christ and his disciples as an embattled warrior group making their last brave stand against a superior enemy force. This model of beleaguered warriors enables the monk to interpret and simplify the complex interrelationship of Christ's opponents—Pharisees, Saducees, the people clamoring for Barabbas, the Roman government—by picturing them all as an attacking army. Judas is described as a deserter and unfaithful knight, but the fleeing of Peter and the other disciples, which surely could be categorized in this warrior analogy as "desertion under fire," causes obvious embarrassment to the author and introduces serious complications.

Nonetheless, depicting Christ as a lord deserted by his retainers and taken prisoner to be held hostage in the stockade of the enemy has an eloquent homiletic benefit: it may actually have occurred to a good portion of the older Saxon noblemen-warriors in his audience who lost their sovereignty to Charlemagne and the Christian Franks. It is perhaps the key to the poetic insight of the *Heliand* that the very military defeat which alienated the audience from *Christianity* serves to establish their closest identity with *Christ*.

The tradition of loyalty to one's lord in battle, defending him even to the point of death, is an ancient one in the Germanic world and was first described by the Roman historian Tacitus seven centuries before the writing of the *Heliand*. With admiration Tacitus described this Germanic tradition and its unique bonding of men into a company as he described the reciprocal relationship between the lord and his men:

> illum defendere, tueri, sua quoque fortia facta gloriae eius adsignare praecipuum sacramentum est: principes pro victoria pugnant, comites pro principe.
>
> *to defend and protect him and to have their deeds of strength add to his glory is particularly sacred to them: the lords fight for victory, the warrior companions fight for the lord.*[1]

The importance of this group cohesion for social stability in a world without departments of justice and unified police organizations may be difficult for us to imagine, but it must have been an effective tradition for as many years before Tacitus as it lasted after him. We know that the ideals of the *comitatus* (i.e., retinue, companions) were still greatly influencing the secular and religious imagination of St. Ignatius Loyola in the sixteenth century. In the ninth century of the *Heliand* monk, it was a tradition that he obviously relished. The nature of the *comitatus* has been summarized as follows:

> The Germanic *comitatus* was a group of men who (1) were (voluntarily) attached to a certain chieftain, thereby creating a bond between the chieftain and each retainer and among all the various retainers as a collective. This group (2) provided glory and honor for its chosen chieftain, and to a certain extent for itself, in both peace and war. (3) Their primary function, however, was on the battlefield, where they fought to the death if necessary for their chosen leader.[2]

That this third element of the tradition was fully alive in the minds of his Saxon audience seems to have been taken for granted by the *Heliand* author. As he retells the story, when the time comes to begin describing the final journey to Jerusalem, many of the apostles begin telling Christ that it is dangerous to go back to the city where he was almost stoned to death. What is described in John's Gospel by a single verse: "Thomas, called the Twin, said to his fellow disciples, 'Let us go, that we may die with him'" (John 11:16) is expanded in the *Heliand* to ten verses:

> Thuo en thero tueliƀio
> Thuomas gimalda—was in githungan mann
> diurlic drohtines thegan—: "ne sculun wi im thia dad lahan," quathie
> "ni wernian wi im thes willien, ac wita im wonian mid,
> thuolonian mid usson thiodne: that is thegenes cust,
> that hie mid is frahon samad fasto gistande,
> doie mid im thar an duome. Duan us alla so,
> folgon im te thero ferdi: ni latan use fera wiđ thiu
> wihtes wirđig, neƀa wi an them werode mid im
> doian mid uson drohtine. Than leƀot us thoh duom after,
> guod word for gumon." (XLVIII, 3992–4002)

Scott translates:

> *Then, one of the twelve,*
> *Thomas, did speak—he was truly an excellent man,*
> *a loyal thane of his lord. "Let us never reproach his deeds,"*

quoth he, "nor reproach his will. But rather we should remain with him,
should suffer with our lord. For that is the choice of a thane:
that he standeth steadfast with his liege together,
doth die with him at his doom. Let us all do so therefore;
let us follow his path, nor let our lives
be worth aught against his, unless we may die
in this host with our lord. So honor will live after us,
a good word before the kinships of men."

The *Heliand* author is not only familiar in detail with *thegenes cust*, but he seizes upon the almost sole opportunity in the Gospel where a disciple promises to stay with Christ in the coming confrontation with the authorities. The *Heliand* does not conceal the fact that among the Twelve was a "treasonous knight" nor does it conceal that "the great swordsman" (Peter) denied his liege three times and that the apostles, including Thomas, "fled in the presence of the enemy." The author casts all these events in what must have been the familiar poetry of the Saxon epic, where the desertion of the hero by his retainers may well have been an all-too-common tragic theme, if we can judge from the small body of Anglo-Saxon literature that has come down to us. The desertion of Christ by his retinue, therefore, becomes not a stumbling block to faith nor a cause of scandal among the Saxons, but a familiar epic event. The author even gives a knightly explanation for Judas's desertion that underscores why his faithlessness was far graver than that of Peter and the others: Peter and the disciples may have failed their lord, but they did not conspire to hand him over to the enemy. Judas is described thus at the Last Supper:

So tho the treulogo
that mos antfeng endi mid is muđu anbet,
so afgaf ia tho thiu godes craft, gramon in gewitun
an thene lichamon, leđa wihti,
warđ imu Satanas sero bitengi,
hardo umbi is herte, siđur ine thiu helpe godes
farlet an thesemu liohte. So is thena liudio we,
the so undar thesemu himile scal herron wehslon.

(LV,4620–27)

When the betrayer
took the food and was eating it in his mouth,
the divine power left him; evil things went
into his body, horrible creatures,
Satan wrapped himself
tightly around his heart, since the help of God
had abandoned him in this world. Thus shall those people suffer,
who, under heaven, change lords.

In *Beowulf*, which may antedate the *Heliand* by one hundred years or more, we can hear Wiglaf's call to the retainers to stand with their lord in his hour of need in much the same tone heard by the author of the *Heliand*:

Wiglaf mađelode word-rihta fela
saegde gesiđum–him waes sefa geomor
"Ic đaet moel geman þaer we medu þegun
þonne we geheton ussum hlaforde
in bior-sele đe us đas beagas geaf
þaet we him đa guđ-getawa gyldan woldon
gif him þislicu þearf gelumpe,
helmas ond heard sweord. Đe he usic on herge geceas
to þyssum siđ-fate sylfes willum,
onmunde usic maerđa...

"Nu is se daeg cumen
þaet ure man-dryhten maegenes behofad,
godra guđ-rinca; wutun gongan to
helpan hild-fruman, þenden hyt sy,
gled-egesa grim! God wat on mec
þaet me is micle leofre þaet minne lic-haman
mid minne gold-gyfan gled faeđmie..."
Wod þa þurh þone wael-rec wig-heafolan baer
frean on fultum... (2631–62)

Wiglaf spoke in sorrow of soul
with bitter reproach rebuking his comrades:
"I remember the time, as we drank in the mead-hall,

when we swore to our lord who bestowed these rings
that we would repay for the war gear and armor,
the hard swords and helmets, if need like this
should ever befall him. He chose us out
from all the host for this high adventure,
deemed us worthy..."

"Now is the day that our lord has need
of the strength and courage of stalwart men.
Let us haste to succor his sore distress
in the horrible heat and the merciless flame.
God knows I had rather the fire should enfold
my body and limbs with my gold-friend and lord..."
Then Wiglaf dashed through the deadly reek
in his battle helmet to help his lord.'[3]

Wiglaf came alone for, although twelve men had accompanied Beowulf on his journey to fight the dragon, all fled except Wiglaf. The epic tradition acknowledged both loyalty to and flight from the lord in his time of danger, something both the Anglo-Saxon tradition and the Gospel story agree on, making it possible for the *Heliand* author to tell the story as it was while using a battle analogy.

The *Battle of Maldon* is a fragmentary poem about a Viking attack on England that occurred in 991 A.D., and is thus many years subsequent to the *Heliand*. The stirring ending of the fragment reveals, however, that the *comitatus/gisiđi* ideals were still vibrantly alive as well as the tragic situation of some men abiding with and some abandoning their lord in his hour of need. The battle is almost lost to the Vikings but the old warrior Byrhtwold reminds the younger warriors of the ancient *thegenes cust*:

Byrhtwold maþelode, bord hafenode
(se waes eald geneat), aesc acwehte;
he ful baldlice beornas laerde:
"Hige sceal þe heardra, heorte þe cenre,
mod sceal þe mare, þe ure maegen lytlađ.
Her lio ure ealdor eall forheawen,
god on greote. A maeg gnornian

se đe nu fram þis wigplegan wendan benceđ.
Ic eom frod feores; fram ic ne wille,
ac ic me be healfe minum hlaforde,
be swa leofan men, licgan þence."

Swa hi Aeþelgares bearn ealle bylde,
Godric to guþe. Oft he gar forlet,
waelspere windan on þa wicingas,
swa he on þam folce fyrmest eode,
heow and hynde, ođþaet he on hilde gecranc.
Naes þaet na se Godric þe đa guđe forbeah.

Byrhtwold encouraged them brandishing buckler,
aged companion shaking ash-spear;
Stout were the words he spoke to his men:
"Heart must be braver, courage the bolder,
mood the stouter as our strength grows less!
Here on the ground my good lord lies
gory with wounds. Always will he regret it
who now from this battle thinks to turn back.
I am old in years; I will never yield,
but here at the last beside my lord,
by the leader I love I think to lie."

And Godric to battle heartened them all;
Aethelgor's son hurled many a spear
At the Viking horde. First in the front
he hacked and hewed till he fell in the slaughter
he was not the Godric who fled from the fight.[4]

The poem did not end with this last line no doubt, but the last line as we have it is as significant as is Byrhtwold's *gesiđi/comitatus* loyalty.

Peter is the knight-companion on whom the *Heliand* author has lavished careful attention to make him an acceptable model for the Saxon warrior noble. He now depicts Peter's behavior, good and bad, during the final battle of his lord, as warrior-retainer behavior.

Peter's conduct at the Last Supper, in which he promised to remain with Christ even if all the others deserted him, is made for our author's purpose.

The Old High German *Tatian* has the following:

Tho antlingita Petrus, quad imo: "into oba sie
alle bisuihane werdent in thir, ih nio in altere
ni wirdu bisuihan, thie dar mit dir garo bin oda in
carkeri oda in tod zi faranne: mina sela sezzu furi thih."
(CLVI,3)

Then Peter answered and said to him: "Even if all
the others are scandalized in you, I will never be
scandalized in you; I am ready to go with you into
prison or to death: I will risk my soul for you."

When one thinks of the speech of Byrhtwold in the *Battle of Maldon*, one almost foresees the few slight changes that would have to be made to alter Peter's speech from a militant one to the familiar military one of Germanic tradition:

Simon Petrus tho
thegan wiđ is thiodan thristwordun sprac
bi huldi wiđ is herron: "thoh thi all thit helido folc,"
quathie,
"gisuican thina gisiđos, thoh ik sinnon mid thi
at allon tharaƀon tholoian williu.
Ik bium garo sinnon, ef mi god latiđ,
that ik an thinon fullestie fasto gistande
thoh sia thi an carcaries clustron hardo
thesa liudi bilucan thoh is mit luttil tueho
ne ik an them bendion mid thi bidan willie,
liggian mid thi so lieƀen; ef sia thines libes than
thuru eggia niđ ahtian williad,
from min thie guodo, ik giƀu min ferah furi thik
an wapno spil: nis mi werđ iowiht
te bimiđanne, so lango so mi min warod
hugi endi handcraft." (LVI,4673–88)

Then Simon Peter,

the noble warrior, graciously spoke confident words
to his Sovereign and Lord. "Even if this entire group of heroes," he said
"your retainers, should flee, I am willing to suffer
any hardships together with you always.
I am always ready and willing, if God lets me,
to help you, to remain standing at your side without wavering.
Even if these people lock you up in the prison's dark dungeon,
I have no doubt
that I will stay with you in chains,
lying with you whom I love so much. If they then want,
with the blade's hatred, to take away your life,
my good Lord, then I will give my life for you
in the play of weapons; and I will not give ground
as long as my courage lasts and my arm has its strength."

I do not think it is necessary to assume that the author of the *Battle of Maldon* fragment was familiar with the *Heliand*. He may have been, but the striking similarity of "I will not give ground as long as my courage lasts and my arm has its strength" and "Heart must be braver, courage the bolder, / mood the stouter as our strength grows less" cannot be ignored. It shows such a high value placed on loyalty unto death that the Christian author simply had to find a way to incorporate it into the final scenes of the Gospel. He had two choices: St. John, who remained under the cross—the only one of the apostles to do so—and St. Peter, who drew his sword to defend Christ and then "fled the battlefield." It is a compliment to the *Heliand* author's unflinching fidelity both to the epic Germanic tradition and the Gospel story that he picked the latter.

The final "battle" begins with Christ himself in the agony in the garden. The *Heliand* does not conceal the human agony, but admits that the Savior was afraid:

was imu is hugi drobi
bi theru menniski mod gihrorid,
is flesk was an forhtun: fellun imo trahni,

drop is diurlic suet, al so dror kumid
wallan fan wundun. (LVII,4748–52)

For his spirit was grieved
and his heart was moved by his humanness.
His flesh feared indeed; tears fell from Him
His dear, precious sweat did drip, even as blood doth drip,
Doth well from a wound. (Scott, p. 163)

The insertion of the tears increases the concrete nature of the fear, but the apparently casual simile—"as blood comes welling out of wounds"—suggests warfare. The *Heliand* turns the Savior's statement of acceptance of his end into a delightfully Germanic one with the sparest of means.

Tatian:

Pater mi, si non potest calix hic transire,
nisi bibam illum, fiat voluntas tua.
Min fater, oba ni mag these kelih furifaran
nibih in trinke, wese thin willo. (182,2)

Father, if this chalice cannot pass away unless I
drink it, then your will be done.

Heliand:

It si than thin willeo so
ik williu is than gicoston: ik nemu thene kelik an hand,
drinku ina thi te diurđu, drohtin fro min,
mahtig mundboro. (LVII,4763–66)

If you want it to be this way,
then I want to drink it: I take this chalice in my hand
and drink it to your honor, my lord chieftain,
powerful protector.

Christ is depicted as lifting up the cup of his suffering and death, holding it in salute to his sovereign and drinking it *thi te diurđu* 'to your honor'. The Jewish metaphor of the act of drinking to mean personal acceptance of something has been transformed by one phrase into a Germanic drinking gesture of salute to one's liege lord, ***drohtin fro min, mahtig mundboro.*** Having made his last salute, Christ wakes his retainers and they see the enemy warriors approaching, marching up the hill carrying their weapons:

> Gesiđos Cristes
> wacodun tho aftar them wordun endi gisahun tho that werod kuman
> an thene berg uppen brahtmu thiu mikilon,
> wreda wapanberand. (LVII,4807–10)

> *The warrior-companions of Christ*
> *were awake after those words and they saw warriors coming*
> *up the hill with a great noise,*
> *angry armed men.*

The structure of the following scene is approximately the same as in *Tatian*. The beginning shows the enemy forces marching up the hill to take Christ prisoner; the last shows them marching down the hill with him into the valley and back up to Fort Jerusalem *fan themu berge te burg* 'from hill to fort'. The central scene, however, is altered so as to give the limelight to Peter as well as to Christ. The phrase of rebuke said to Peter, "Should I not drink the cup which the Father has given me?", has been omitted, as it would have to be, granted the altered interpretation given to the image of drinking the cup in the agony in the garden. Omitted alson, presumably as something unthinkable for a Germanic lord's retinue, is Jesus' request that his disciples be allowed to go free. The disciples in the *Heliand*, surprisingly, do not ask if they should strike with the sword *'si percutimus in gladio? / Oba wir slahemes in suerte'* (*Tatian*:185,1), but rather ask much more fatalistically if it is their lord's will that they also be impaled on spears *'that sie us her an speres ordun spildien mostin'* (LVIII,4862). If so, they will be glad to suffer it. This verse is troublesome. It is not present in *C* and seems to presuppose a Latin manuscript of *Tatian* or one of the altar Gospels in which the above *percutimus* (1st plural *active*) was miscopied or misunderstood by the Heliand author as *percutimur* (1st plural *passive*), thus changing the disciples' question from "should we strike" to "should we be struck?"

Nonetheless, the appropriateness of passivity in the face of the final events is made quite clear in song fifty-eight of the *Heliand*. Even Christ on the top of the Mount of Olives, waiting for the enemy to come up, is described in good fatalistic style as merely standing there with his disciples awaiting the workings of Fate *'bed metodogiskapu'* (LVIII,4827). The Gospel account says that Jesus rebuked the disciples for falling asleep; in the *Heliand*, Jesus adds: *Thiu wurd is at handun / that it so gigangen scal, so it god fader / gimarcode mahtig* (LVIII,4778–80) 'Fate is at hand so that it will happen as God the Father powerfully planned it.' After he tells Peter to put up his sword since "he who lives by the sword will perish by the sword," Christ adds a more sober, Germanic reason: *wi mid usun dadiun ni sculun/wiht awerdian* (LVIII, 4899–4900) 'we cannot by our deeds avert anything.' Peter is the exception:

> Tho gibolgan warđ snel suerdthegan, Simon Petrus,
> well imu innan hugi, that he ni mahte enig word sprekan:
> so harm warđ imu an is hertan, that man is herron thar
> binden welde. Tho he gibolgan geng,
> suiđo thristmod thegan for is thiodan standen,
> hard for is herron: ni was imu is hugi tuifli,
> blođ an is breaston, ac he is bil atoh,
> suerd bi sudu, slog imu tegegnes
> an thene furiston fiund folmo crafto
> that tho Malchus warđ makeas eggiun
> an thea suiđaron half suerdu gimalod:
> thiu hlust warđ imu farhauwan, he warđ an that hođid wund
> that imu herudrorag hlear endi ore
> beniwundun brast: blod aftar sprang
> well fan wunden. Tho was an is wangun scard
> the furisto thero fiundo. Tho stod that folc an rum:
> andredun im thes billes biti. (LVIII,4865–82)

> *Then he got really angry,*
> *Simon Peter, the mighty, noble swordsman,*
> *his mind was so upset, that he couldn't speak a single word:*
> *his heart became bitter, because they wanted to tie up*

his lord there. So he moved angrily,
that determined noble warrior, to stand in front of his liege lord,
right in front of his lord. No doubting in his mind,
no hesitation in his chest—he drew his steel blade,
the sword at his side, and struck straight ahead
at the first man of the enemy, with all his hand's strength,
so that Malchus was cut and wounded on the right side by the sword:
his ear was chopped off, he was so badly wounded in the head
that his cheek and ear
burst open with a mortal wound; blood gushed out,
pouring from the wound. The cheek of the enemy's first man
had been cut open. The people around stood back–
they were afraid of the slash of the sword.

This passage is probably the most cited in the *Heliand*. Peter is given one moment of glory to show what a warrior he was. The author improves on the somewhat superficial nature of the wound in the Gospel harmony *amputavit auriculam eius dextram / abahio sin ora thaz zesewa* 'he cut off his right ear' (185,2) and makes it far more serious, including half of poor Malchus's face. Malchus is not a mere servant of the high priest but, if he stood facing Peter when Peter was standing in front of Christ, then Malchus must have been *thene furiston fiund* 'the first man of the enemy.' More important for Peter's stature is the shock effect of his swordplay. Peter is made here almost equal with Christ in that his sword has the same effect of making the crowd fall back as does the Savior's voice when he tells them, "It is I."

In the *Heliand*, I believe the author is more than aware of the theatrics he ascribes to Peter. Christ is unhesitatingly depicted as being taken, made a prisoner of war, and of telling Peter the traditional words, "those who live by the sword..." as well as the additional phrase, "we cannot by our deeds avert anything." Like Beowulf and Byrhtwold, Christ is shown teaching Peter the parallelism of two of the oldest Germanic and Christian religious attitudes: calm acceptance of the unavoidable and submission to the will of God.

As the Savior is taken prisoner the German scholar may hear echoes of one of the oldest known texts in the Germanic languages—an ancient plea for the release of captives from their bonds through the intercession of the gods. It is expressed in the *Merseburger Zaubersprüche.*

Eiris sazun idisi, sazun hera duoder
suma hapt heptidun, suma heri lezidun
suma clubodun umbi cuoniouwidi:
inspring haptbandun, invar vigandun.

Once women [Valkyries?] sat there–the armies everywhere,
some held by bonds, some being wounded by the armies,
some clawing at their sacred fetters:
escape from the bonds, run away from the enemy![5]

Jesus joins the generations of those made prisoners of war in the Germanic countries by a simple phonetic allusion to this old magic formula recited for their freedom.

Heftun herubendium handi tesamne
fađmos mid fitereun.

They locked his hands together with military
handcuffs and his arms with chain. (4917–18)

The Saxon nobles are perhaps being gently assisted to accept the unpalatable defeat in their own past and present. Their sufferings, perhaps even the sounds of their pagan prayers for freedom, are incorporated into the Gospel story as the Fate of Christ. The deftness of this simple allusion may be seen by contrasting it with the words of the *Tatian*:

Fiengun then heilant into buntun inan. (185,10)

They seized Jesus and bound him.

What now of Peter? Judas was castigated for having changed lords under heaven, but the Lord's other warrior–Peter–also fled and denied his liege even if he did not change his fealty. To rescue his model disciple for the Saxons, the *Heliand* author goes to some length to explain how "this dear man," the "mighty swordsman," the "best of warriors" could have denied his lord three times at the word of a serving girl. The author's explanation is both endearing spiritually and satisfying sociopolitically. It was to prepare *Peter* to be a mild (i.e., kind and generous) warrior-king. In an excursus with no parallel in the Gospel, the author explains that Peter's denials were: (a) what God wanted and, therefore, like a fated doom, unavoidable: *it weldi god* (LIX,5024) 'God wanted it'; (b) done on behalf of the people that God might have a ruler over his household who personally understands human frailty: *let ina gekunnon, huilke craft habet / the mennisca mod ano the maht godes* (LIX,5031–32) 'to let him realize how much of strength there is in human intentions, and how much there is in the power of God'; (c) so that Peter, as ruler, would be more able to appreciate how people love to be forgiven when they have done something wrong, and that he would more easily forgive: *so im tho selƀo dede / hebenriki god harmgewurhti* (LIX,5037–39) 'just as the God of heaven forgave him the wrong he had done'.

Christ himself is treated throughout the passion account as a handcuffed prisoner of war being subjected to torture. One cannot but be impressed both by the minimal amount of adjusting of the original text that this interpretation of the story requires. Christ before Pontius Pilate is easily imaged as a prisoner of war bravely facing the enemy: *stod that barn godes / fast under fiundun: warun im is fađmos gebundene* (LXI,5117–18) 'the Child of God stood fast surrounded by the enemy, his arms were tied'. He was handed over by the Jews into the hands of the enemy: *under fiundo folc* (LXI,5134), saying that he should be executed at swordpoint: *wapnes eggiun/scarpun scurun* (LXI,5135–36) 'with the weapon's edge, by the sharp sword'. There is no mention at this point of crucifixion. Still more interesting is the repeated insistence that the rulers causing this captivity and torture all come from Caesar and Rome. Pilate is introduced as *bodo fan Rumuburg* (LXI,5125) 'legate from Fort Rome' and *kuman was he fan themu Kesure... to rihtiene that riki* (LXI,5127–28) 'coming from Caesar... to rule that realm,' even before his name is mentioned. This point, repeated again and again regarding Pilate and Herod, was not lost on the Saxons who, at the time of the writing, were being ruled by the legates of the Holy Roman "Caesar."

The author is now faced with the problem of the crucifixion and the death of Christ. Having gone to such lengths to create an identity between the Saxons and Peter, between the Saxons and Christ the captive, he now must face a depressing termination: Christ and the Saxons losing the last battle to Fate, to the Romans, to death? Would not even the resurrection seem to be something tacked on, something that could not be fitted into the battle analogy? The *Heliand* presents an ingenious solution to the problem. First, Fate approaches Christ and the Passion and Death begin, but *wurd* is called God's glorious might. Second, there is no resort to any other Germanic model, such as Valkyries bringing the fallen warrior to heaven. The author stays with his allegorical war model. The death of Christ is brilliantly treated as an *escape* of a prisoner of war from his captors, and the resurrection as the return of the warrior leader to his own people. The enemy from whom Christ escapes is transformed from the Roman army to death itself.

In Song sixty-four, *wurd* and *metod* begin to approach after the Jews successfully intimidate Caesar's legate into giving up his first attempt to release the prisoner. The author has explained in an aside that Christ could not let the Jews know he was the Son of God for fear they would lose heart about putting him to death–and then the kingdom of heaven would not be opened to the sons of man. The *Heliand* continues:

> Thiu wurd nahida thuo
> mari maht godes endi middi dag,
> that sia thia ferahquala frummian scoldun. (LXIV,5394–96)

> *Then Fate approached,*
> *the great power of God, and noon approached*
> *so that they should carry out the agonies of death.*

Here both Fate and time are almost personified manifestations of the power of God. Thus they can approach God's Son without being considered a hostile force. Christ's real enemy is not these ancient powers but Satan. The *Heliand* author seems aware of how appropriate that is. Satan "the enemy" surfaces in song sixty-five wearing a Germanic *Tarnkappe* to try to frustrate the Fate of Christ. The *Tarnkappe* (*helidhelm* in the *Heliand*) was a mythic hood or cloak that rendered its wearer invisible. It plays a prominent if somewhat disreputable role in several of the marital scenes in the *Nibelungenlied*. The *Heliand* author describes the brief attempt by Pilate's wife to stop her husband's involvement in the condemnation of Christ ("have nothing to do with this just man, for I have suffered much in a dream on his account") as an attempt by Satan to stop Fate from bringing about the saving death of Christ. This reinforces the combining of Fate with the power of God. The reinterpretation of the episode with Pilate's wife may have been borrowed by the *Heliand* monk from his abbot, because we can read the same theological interpretation of Pilate's wife's attempt at intervention in Rabanus Maurus's commentary on Matthew.[6] The combining of this opposition to the crucifixion with resistance to Fate, the power of God, is, I believe, the poet's own.

As the crucifixion occurs there is the familiar gentle shading of the picture with Germanic religious imagery. The god who won wisdom for the world by his suffering did so, as we have seen, hanging from the cosmic tree at the axis of the world. Christ's cross is initially described as being erected like a gallows from which he is to be hung but, once it is standing, it is called a *tree* on the mountain—and that image is put in the climactic position of the first clause of song sixty-six:

> Thuo sia thar an griete galgon rihtun,
> an them felde uppan folc Iudeono,
> bome an berege. (5532–34)

> *There on the sandy gravel they erected the gallows*
> *up on the field, the Jewish people set it up,*
> *a tree on the mountain.*

Thus the forgiving of the enemy soldiers, *huand sia ni witun, huat sia duot* 'since they know not what they do', a Christian doctrine that almost surely must have rubbed the Saxons the wrong way, is persuasively placed in the context of Wodenic wisdom. Even the suffering on the cross, without any attempt to get blood-vengeance, is depicted as perhaps not all that foreign to the worshipers of Woden. It even takes place on the familiar sandy gravel of the North Sea shore.

As the bones of the two thieves are broken, Christ escapes. The soldiers come to break his legs but Christ has already died of the wounds suffered in battle and death provided him with his escape from the ropes of captivity. This supplied a perfect image for the defeated and captive Saxons.

> "Ik an thina hendi befilhu," quathie,
> "minon gest an godes willion; hie ist nu garo te thiu
> fus te faranne." Firiho drohtin
> gihnegida thuo is hobid, helagon ađom
> liet fan themo likhamen. So thuo thie landes ward
> sualt an them simon...
>
> fundun ina gifaranan thuo iu:
> is seola was gisendid an suođan weg
> an langsam lioht, is liđi cuoloden
> that ferah was af them fleske.
> (LXVII,5654–58 and 5700–5703)
>
> *"Into your hands," he said, "I commend*
> *my spirit to the will of God; my spirit is ready*
> *to go to you, ready to travel." The lord of mankind*
> *then bowed his head, the holy breath*
> *escaped from the body. As the land's ruler*
> *died in the ropes... [or "(hanging) from the rope"]*
>
> *They found him already gone:*
> *his shade had been sent on the true road*
> *to the long-lasting light, his body's limbs cooled,*
> *his conscious spirit was far from the flesh.*

The *Heliand* poet describes the burial of Christ's body in as heroic terms as the Gospel text will permit. Joseph of Arimathea, a true if secret knight of Christ, takes the body down from the cross and, with a tenderness that reminds one of Beowulf's death scene, takes out the nails and *antfeng ina mid is fađmon, so man is frohon scal, liobes lichamon* (LXVIII, 5733–34) 'took him into his arms, the precious body, as one should do with one's liege-lord'.

Thus some of the expected *comitatus* behavior is found in the account of the burial of Christ. The *Heliand*, in another of its more deft strokes of ambiguity, has Christ buried in a tomb as in the Gospel account. The resurrection, however, is depicted as occurring from under the stone slab of a mound grave. The poem deliberately visualizes the resurrection of Christ in a manner that is in violation of the Carolingian law against burial in pagan (Saxon) mound graves, thus creating an image of Christ risen that gives clear hope of Saxon resurrection.

The resurrection is described as a return of the escaped spirit back into the body. The warriors are keeping watch before the grave in the dark night, sitting under their shields *'bidun undar iro bordon'* (LXVIII,5766) when suddenly bright day comes over the middle realm *'middilgard'*:

Thar ward thie gest cuman be godes crafte,
helag adom undar thena hardon sten
an thena lichamon. (LXVIII,5769–72)

There was the spirit coming, by the power of God,
the holy breath going under the hard stone
to the corpse.

This traveling spirit or shade may not strike us immediately as familiar but its very concreteness may indicate that this image of a moving shade or soul would not surprise the Saxons and may represent another ingenious example of Christian belief being expressed in older pagan forms.[7]

In depicting the Resurrection, the *Heliand* author combines the concept of freedom as the ability to go where one pleases, to escape from captivity, with the image of light.

Lioht was thuo giopanod
firio barnon te frumu: was fercal manag
antheftid fan helldoron endi te himele weg
giwaraht fan thesaro weroldi. Wanom up astuod
fridubarn godes, fuor im thuo thar hie welda...
so huem so ina muosta undar is ogon scawon

so bereht endi so bliđi; all so blicsmun lioht;
was im is giwadi wintarcaldon
snewe gilicost. (LXVIII,5772–76 and LXIX,5807–10)

There light was opened up
for the good of mankind: the locks and bars
were removed from the world of the dead and the road to heaven
from this world was laid down. When God's child of peace
rose up, he could go wherever he wanted...
no one could look up into his eyes
so blindingly brilliant was the light—like a lightning flash;
his garment was like winter-cold
snow.

The author has expanded the nature of liberty from freedom from captivity to the more theological concept of freedom from the ultimate captivity of death. Moreover he has shifted the emphasis from the women at the tomb being startled by the whiteness of the angel's garment to the brilliant white of Christ, and has laid a northern accent on the comparison "whiter than snow", *'sicut nix'* (*Tatian* CLXXIII,3) by strengthening it to "whiter than winter-cold snow" or possibly "whiter than new-fallen snow." In emphasizing the white light of the resurrection in such a striking way, the *Heliand* has made a frame story out of the whole Gospel. The *Heliand* account of the blinding light bursting into the middle realm *'middilgard'* and shocking the soldiers on guard at the tomb reminds one of the parallel scene at the beginning of the epic where Joseph's grooms are watching the horses by night on Christmas Eve and are suddenly blinded by a brilliant light and startled by the angels. Similarly, as in the account of the walking on the water, the *Heliand* clarifies the form structure and creates the inclusion-form structure that one expects in epic poetry. Consequently the transfiguration (XXXVIII), in which the brilliant shining of Christ makes the summit of Mount Tabor seem like paradise itself, is the central scene of the light-structure of this epic, with the powerful scenes of the light of Christmas Eve and the light of Easter morning constituting the two sides of the triptych.[8]

The appearances of Christ to the women follow as well the appearances to Peter and John. The account of the two disciples on the way to Emmaus is incomplete and we are left with but a fragment of the description of the ascension into heaven. Christ is portrayed in standard Gospel terms as raising his hands in blessing over his disciples and ascending into heaven where he is seated on his throne at the right hand of the Father. It is at this point that the *Heliand* attributes to Christ the prime activity formerly reserved to Woden alone: to be seated above, but gazing below and observing all things:

> Sitit imo thar an thea suiđron half godes
> alomahtiges fader endi thanan all gesihit
> waldandeo Crist, so huat so thius werold behabet.
> (LXXI,5976–78)

> *There he is seated forever at the right side of God*
> *the almighty Father and from there he sees all things,*
> *the ruling Christ sees whatever is happening in the world.*

At this point the story, even if not textually complete, is brought to an end. The monk-poet has cleared a gentle path for his Saxons, a path on which they can overcome their conquerors through the very religion brought by the conquerors and, in a real sense, overcome the 'Christians' with Christ. In Christian spirituality they can escape their captivity by the Franks and even rise again to a new life. They need not fear the loss of their knighthood, for the *Heliand* has shown them a new type of *comitatus* loyalty. They also need not fear that they have lost a divinity who calms the waters for them nor even a god who, by suffering on the tree, learned to see the world from his throne in heaven. They have all these things preserved and renewed in the Saxon Savior, the *Heliand*, Jesus Christ.

Within four generations, the first non-Frank came to rule Western Christendom as Holy Roman Emperor. Otto I, a Saxon, ascended the throne of Charlemagne. Who knows how much the unknown poet-monk of the *Heliand* may have helped toward the eventual resurrection—and enthronement—of his people.

Notes

1. Tacitus, *Germania*, XIV.

2. John Lindow, *Comitatus, Individual and Honor* (Berkeley: University of California Press, 1975), p. 11. Lindow concludes that the word *gesiđi* used in the *Heliand* to designate the apostles may have been used in the first century A.D. simply to mean traveling companions. Its technical sense of retainer arose later. Etymologically, he derives the word from **ga-*, equivalent to the Latin *con-* 'with', and the Germanic **sind* 'way, path, direction'. The word thus designates people who 'go together.' I am afraid the nearest contemporary English formation to the oldest Germanic use of the word might well be "gang."

3. Charles W. Kennedy, *An Anthology of Old English Poetry* (New York: Oxford University Press, 1960), pp. 84–85.

4. Ibid., p. 169.

5. Wilhelm Braune, Althochdeutsches Lesebuch (Tübingen: Max Niemeyer Verlag, 1958), p. 86.

6. "[Hac autem vice, non ante,] se intellexerit diabolus per Christi mortem nudandum et spolia humani generis sive in mundo, sive apud tartara amissurum. Et ideo satagebat per mulierem per quam spolia mortis invaserat, Christum eripere de manibus Judaeorum, ne per illius mortem ipse amitteret mortis imperium." [The devil understood that by the death of Christ he would be stripped of his human spoils both in the world and in hell, therefore he sought by means of a woman, since through a woman [Eve] he had usurped death's spoils, to save Christ from the hands of the Jews, so that the devil would not lose control of death's empire by the death of Christ]. B. Rabani Mauri, *Commentariorum in Mattheum Libri Octo*, Lib. VIII, cap. XXVII, p. 1131, in J.-P. Migne, *Patrologia Latina*, vol. 107, (Paris: Migne, 1864).

7. Hans Eggers's philological analysis of concepts for mind and soul finds that *seola* must have originally meant the 'shade' or mysterious moving soul of the dead. He concludes that this pre-Christian meaning is maintained in the *Heliand*: "Die Seele fährt zur Hel, und viele Seelen sind dort versammelt. Daher kann der Dichter auch von Seelen im Plural sprechen. Das ist aber nur möglich, wenn seola ursprünglich den 'Schatten' bedeutete, die

Totenseele, jenes nebelhafte Nachbild des Menschen (*saiwala* = 'die Wallende, Gestaltlose': ein Tabu-Wort?), das nach dem Tode in der Hel sein Dasein führt." See his "Altgermanische Seelenvorstellungen im Lichte des Heliand," *Niederdeutsches Jahrbuch—Jahrbuch des Vereins für niederdeutsche Sprachforschung*, 80 (1957), 20. (Also in Eichhoff und Rauch, Heliand, pp. 299–300.)

8. Rathofer has arrived at the same conclusion based on his numerical-form analysis of the *fitts*.

AFTERWORD

The *Heliand* is a great achievement in the use of poetry and specifically poetic analogy, to bring about intercultural communication on the highest level: the level of the spiritual. The author's success, I believe, lies in his classic sense of proportion in his creating of poetic equivalencies between northern and Palestinian forms of expression. In almost all cases he chooses the path of doing the absolutely appropriate *minimum* necessary to effect the transformation, and thus never seems guilty of romantic exaggeration.

In changing, for example, the scene of the walking on the water, he does the minimum necessary in order to get the pericope into balanced epic form. In transforming the geography, he does not introduce waves crashing on the shore but simply refers to the sand of the seashore. When answering the statement: "What is salt worth if it loses its taste?", he simply adds "it becomes as useless as the salt on the seashore, which people walk on."

His light but perfect touch is perhaps most poignantly seen in the transforming of the gesture of drinking the cup of suffering, in the agony in the garden scene, into one of lifting the cup as a soldier's last salute to his lord. A minimum of transformation of the image in the text and a powerful cultural equivalent is created and seen.

The author's touching treatment of the difficult matter of the eight Beatitudes and his masterfully moving version of the Lord's Prayer stand as evidence of his classical sensitivity to the degree of change required to bring the meaning of the text across cultures in a moving way. The changing of the phrase "hallowed be thy name" by the simple and minimal addition of "in every word we speak," not only culturally adapts the text, but also suddenly restores life to the original by lifting it from the level of cliché to the level of a phrase with meaning.

The *Heliand* author also possesses the same gentle but sure feel in dealing with the religious feelings and images of his own people. He does not reprove, but again and again puts the phrase "do not let your minds doubt" into the mouths and descriptions of his most heroic characters. On the other hand, the religious sentiments of his people: the fear of Fate, limits, time, are given ample expression in his Gospel. With a sure hand he neither places these entities of the old religion so low as to be insulting to the Saxons and their ancestors, nor so high as to be threatening to the divine status of the Father, Son, and Holy Spirit of the new religion. He still leaves the old powers in place but delineates their powers to control the timing of natural events within the overall framework of the Christian religion. And for those who miss the old iconography, he has lowered the traditional position of the Dove above Christ just enough so that it is sitting in a more familiar position on the new God of wisdom's shoulder.

Even politically the *Heliand* author shows his deep sense of proper balance. While identifying the Saxons with Christ and Peter, and associating the Franks with Caesar and Rome, he lets the good and bad of the status quo stand, and does not turn his work into political propaganda for one side or the other. He holds up the mirror to the tragic situation as it exists, repeats and emphasizes Christ's warning to Peter about putting the sword back into its sheath, by adding his own moderate and Germanic reason: "what can we avert by our deeds?" With a wisdom perhaps even beyond his intent, by counseling closer identification with the Fate of Christ and his men, he enabled his Saxons to eventually adopt not just Christianity but to make Christendom their own.

Two anomalies in the text that have appeared in this study may be of use to philologically oriented scholars. The first is the mistaken use of the Holy Spirit rather than the Son as the divine Person who became incarnate in Christ. This might possibly point to a text and monastery where there was a mistaken verson of the Creed or Gospel in use. It could also, however, be a simple error on the poet's part.

The second anomaly fits the possible reading of the *r* for *s* in the phrase ***si percutimus in gladio*** 'should we strike with the sword' in a text being read by the *Heliand* author. Once again if a Gospel text of appropriate age can be found in which the *s* in *percutimus* is an *r*, or could be easily be read as an *r*, then we might possibly be able to identify an actual text which the author was using.

A final word. The effect of the *Heliand* in its day may well have been much greater than has been acknowledged. The diverse numbers of fragments that have survived is evidence of this, as is the rise of medieval culture itself centered on the very powerful synthesis of northern warrior culture and the Christian Gospel. This synthesis was first made, and made effectively, in the *Heliand*. Previous expressions of the Christian as "warrior" do indeed go back as far as St. Paul who, in Ephesians 6:10–17, refers to Christians as having to put on "the armor of God" and "the breastplate of justice," to take up "the shield of faith" and to take unto themselves "the helmet of salvation" and "the sword of the spirit." Nowhere, however, is the entire Gospel of Christ himself transformed into such terms, and nowhere is the "Fate" of Christ and his "warriors" used as the poetic explanation for the calling and teaching of the disciples and for the description of the entire passion, death, and resurrection scenes of Christ himself. This is powerful culture-creating stuff, and may indeed be *the* poetic source for the high culture of the Middle Ages which would eventually, and ironically, come to idealize Charlemagne in its light; a Saxon-containing culture that could then, equally ironically, march off in Christian warfare against stubborn nonbelievers to the East. The imagery is still known: "Onward Christian Soldiers."

The final achievement of the *Heliand*, though, lies in itself and in the amazing effect it still has on readers who are a long way removed from ninth-century Saxony and medieval Europe. The *Heliand* still touches us because its author rises to brilliance as his humane spirit and compassionate heart, confronted with two cultures in conflict, sought to create a harmony between them. The *Heliand* poet was gifted with a love of both these cultures and refused to choose between them. With his love and poetry he was able to bring these cultures into a stunning and peaceful communion by reimagining the entire Christian Gospel in Saxon northern Europe. Thanks in great part to him, I believe, the Gospel came to feel at home in the North and stayed there "unto this very day."

SELECT BIBLIOGRAPHY

Primary Sources

Heliand und Genesis. Herausgegeben von Otto Behaghel, 8. Auflage bearbeitet von Walther Mitzka. Tübingen: Max Niemeyer Verlag, 1965. Also: 9. Auflage bearbeitet von Burkhard Taeger. Tübingen: Max Niemeyer Verlag, 1984.

Tatian, Lateinisch und Altdeutsch mit ausführlichem Glossar. Herausgegeben von Eduard Sievers. 2. neubearbeitete Ausgabe. Paderborn: Ferdinand Schöningh, 1966.

Secondary Sources

Alexander, Michael. *The Earliest English Poems.* Berkeley and Los Angeles: University of California Press, 1970.

Anderson, Theodore M. "The Caedmon fiction in the Heliand preface." *PMLA*, 89 (1974), 278–284.

Baetke, Walter. *Vom Geist und Erbe Thules.* Göttingen: Vandenhoeck, 1944. See especially "Die Aufnahme des Christentums durch die Germanen," 82–105.

Becker, Gertraud. *Geist und Seele im Altsächsischen und im Althochdeutschen; der Sinnbereich des Seelischen und die Wörter gest-geist und seola-sela in den Denkmälern bis zum 11. Jahrhundert.* Heidelberg: C. Winter Universitätsverlag, 1964.

Bede's Ecclesiastical History of the English People. Ed. Bertram Colgrave and R.A.B. Mynors. Oxford: Clarendon Press, 1969.

Belkin, Johanna, and Jürgen Meier. *Bibliographie zu Otfrid von Weissenburg und zur altsächsischen Bibeldichtung (Heliand und Genesis).* Berlin: E. Schmidt, 1975.

Beowulf. [Reproduced in facsimile from the unique manuscript British Museum MS. Cotton Vitellius A. XV, transliteration and notes by Julius Zupitza.] London and New York: Oxford University Press, 1959.

Berr, Samuel. *An Etymological Glossary to the Old Saxon Heliand.* Bern and Frankfurt: Herbert Lang, 1971.

Bischoff, Bernhard. "Die Schriftheimat der Münchener Heliand-Handschrift" in *Beiträge zur Geschichte der deutschen Sprache und Literatur* 101. Tübingen: Max Niemeyer Verlag, 1979, 161ff.

Bonifatii Epistolae; Willibaldi Vita Bonifatii. Editionem Curavit Reinholdus Rau. Darmstadt: Wissenschaftliche Buchgesellschaft, 1968.

Bostock, J. Knight. *A Handbook on Old High German Literature.* Second Edition, revised by K. C. King and D. R. McLintock. Oxford: Clarendon Press, 1976.

Braune, Wilhelm. *Althochdeutsches Lesebuch.* Tübingen: Max Niemeyer Verlag, 1958.

Bretschneider, Anneliese. *Die Heliandheimat und ihre sprachgeschichtliche Entwicklung.* Marburg: Elwert, 1934.

Carolingian Chronicles: Royal Frankish Annals and Nithard's Histories. Trans. Bernhard Walter Scholz with Barbara Rogers. Ann Arbor: University of Michigan Press, 1972.

Davidson, H. R. Ellis. *Gods and Myths of Northern Europe.* Harmondsworth: Penguin Books, 1964.

De Boor, Helmut. *Die deutsche Literatur: Von Karl dem Großen bis zum Beginn der Höfischen Dichtung, 770-1170.* 5. Auflage. Munich: C.H. Beck'sche Verlagsbuchhandlung, 1962.

Du Four, Xavier Leon. "Jesus' Understanding of His Death," *Theology Digest* 24 (Fall 1976), 293–300.

Ebrard, Johann Heinrich August. *Die iroschottische Missionskirche des sechsten, siebenten und achten Jahrhunderts und ihre Verbreitung und Bedeutung auf dem Festland.* Hildesheim and New York: Georg Olms Verlag, 1971. (Reprint of the 1873 Gütersloh edition.)

Eggers, Hans. "Altgermanische Seelenvorstellungen im Lichte des Heliands" *Jahrbuch des Vereins für niederdeutsche Sprachforschung*, 80 (1957), 1–24.

Eichhoff, Jürgen and Irmengard Rauch. *Der Heliand.* Darmstadt: Wissenschaftliche Buchgesellschaft, 1973.

Einhard, *The Life of Charlemagne*, translated from the *Monumenta Germaniae* by Samuel Epes Turner. Ann Arbor: University of Michigan Press, 1960.

Foerste, William. "Otfrieds literarisches Verhältnis zum Heliand." *Niederdeutsches Jahrbuch*, 71/73 (1950), 40–67.

Friesse, E. R. "The Beginnings of the Heliand." *Modern Language Review*, 50 (1955), 55–57.

Genzmer, Felix. *Heliand und die Bruchstücke der Genesis*. Stuttgart: Reclam, 1982.

Göhler, Hulda. "Das Christusbild in Otfrids Evangelienbuch und im Heliand" in *Zeitschrift für deutsche Philologie* 59. Stuttgart: Kohlhammer, 1935, 1–52.

Green, Dennis Howard. *The Carolingian Lord*; Semantic Studies on Four Old High German Words: *balder*, *fro*, *truhtin*, *herro*. Cambridge: University Press, 1965. [An admirable work of exceptional balance and thoroughness.]

Grosch, Elizabeth. "Das Gottes- und Menschenbild im Heliand." *Beiträge zur Geschichte der deutschen Sprache und Literatur* 72 (1950), 90–120.

Hagenlocher, Albrecht. *Schicksal im Heliand; Verwendung und Bedeutung der nominalen Bezeichnungen*. Cologne; Vienna: Bohlau, 1975.

Heffner, R. M. S. "Concerning the Heliand Verses 5-8." *Monatshefte* 56 (1964), 103-5.

Heuss, Walter. "Zur Quellenfrage im Heliand und im althochdeutschen Tatian." *Niederdeutsches Jahrbuch*, 77 (1954), 1–6.

Hodgkins, Thomas. *Charles the Great*. Port Washington, N.Y.: Kennikat Press, 1970.

Huber, Wolfgang. *Heliand und Matthäusexegese: Quellenstudien insbesondere zu Sedulius Scotus*. Munich: Hueber, 1969.

Kennedy, Charles W. *An Anthology of Old English Poetry*. New York: Oxford University Press, 1960.

Krogmann, Willy. "Crist III und Heliand" in Festschrift für Ludwig Wolff zum 80. Geburtstag. Hrsg. von Werner Schröder. Neumünster: Wachholtz, 1962, 111–19.

Landström, Bjorn. *The Ship, An Illustrated History*. Garden City, N.Y.: Doubleday, 1967.

Leges Saxonum und Lex Thuringorum (Fontes Iuris Germanici Antiqui in Usum Scholarum ex Monumentis Germaniae Historicis Separatim Editi). Harausgegeben von Claudius Freiherrn von

Schwerin. Hannover and Leipzig: Hahnsche Buchhandlung, 1918. [Contains the *Capitulatio de partibus Saxoniae*].

The Letters of St. Boniface. Translated by Ephraim Emerton. New York: Columbia University Press, 1940.

Lindow, John. *Comitatus, Individual and Honor: Studies in North Germanic Institutional Vocabulary.* Berkeley: University of California Press, 1976.

Lintzel, Martin. *Der sächsische Stammesstaat und seine Eroberung durch die Franken.* Berlin: Verlag Dr. Emil Ebering, 1933.

Magnusson, Magnus. *Vikings!* New York: Elsevier-Dutton, 1980.

Masser, Achim. *Bibel und Legendenepik des deutschen Mittelalters.* Berlin: Erich Schmidt Verlag, 1976.

———. "Pilatus im Heliand." *Niederdeutsches Jahrbuch* 96 (1973), 9–17.

Metzenthin, Ernst Christian Paul. *The Home of the Addressees of the Heliand.* Menasha, Wisc.: George Banta, 1922.

Mittner, Ladislaus. *Wurd: das Sakrale in der altgermanischen Epik.* Bern: Francke Verlag, 1955.

Neumann, Friedrich. *Geschichte der altdeutschen Literatur (800–1600).* Berlin: Walter de Gruyter, 1966.

Pertz, Georgius Henricus. *Scriptores Rerum Germanicarum, Ex Monumentis Germaniae Historicis.* Hannover: Hahn, 1865.

Peters, Elizabeth. *Quellen und der Charakter der Paradiesesvorstellungen in der deutschen Dichtung vom 9. bis 12. Jahrhundert.* Breslau: M. and H. Markus, 1915.

Pickering, F. P. "Christlicher Erzählstoff bei Otfried und im Heliand." *Zeitschrift für deutsches Altertum und deutsche Literatur*, 85 (1954–1955), 262-91.

Preisker, Herbert. *Deutsches Christentum; die neutestamentlichen Evangelien im altdeutschen Heliand.* Langensalza; Berlin: Verlag Julius Beltz, 1934.

Priebsch, Robert. *The Heliand Manuscript, Cotton Caligula A. VII in the British Museum, A Study.* Oxford: Clarendon Press, 1925.

Quispel, G. "Some Remarks on the Gospel of Thomas." *New Testament Studies*, 5 (1959), 276–90.

Rabani, Mauri. *Commentariorum in Mattheum Libri Octo*, lib. VIII, cap. XXVII, p. 1131 in J.-P. Migne, *Patrologia Latina*, vol. 107 (Paris: Migne, 1864).

Rathofer, Johannes. *Der Heliand: theologischer Sinn als tektonische Form; Vorbereitung und Grundlegung der Interpretation*. Cologne: Bohlau, 1962.

———. "Hraban und das Petrusbild der 37 Fitte im Heliand." *Festschrift für Jost Trier zum 70 Geburtstag*. Hrsg. von William Foerste und Karl Heinz Borck. Cologne; Graz: Bohlau, 1964, 268–83.

———. "Zum Aufbau des Heliand." *Zeitschrift für deutsches Altertum und deutsche Literatur*, 93 (1964) 239–72. [Also in Eichhoff and Rauch, *Der Heliand*.]

———. "Zum Eingang. Ein textkritischer Versuch im Lichte der Quelle." *Niederdeutsches Wort* 9 (1969), 52–72.

Reed, Carrol. "Gnomic Verse in the Old Saxon Heliand." *Philological Quarterly*, 30 (1951), 403–410.

Robinson, George W. *The Life of St. Boniface by Willibald*. Cambridge: Harvard University Press, 1916.

Robinson, Potter Rodney. *The Germania of Tacitus, A Critical Edition*. Middletown, Conn.: American Philological Association, 1935.

Rompelman, Tom Albert. *Heliandprobleme*. Wilhelmshafen: Schriftenreihe der nordwestdeutschen Universitätsgesellchaft, 1957.

Rupp, Heinz. "The Adoption of Christian Ideas into German, with Reference to the Heliand and Otfrid's 'Evangelienbuch'." *Parergon* 21 (1978), 33–41.

———. "Der Heliand. Hauptanliegen seines Dichters." *Deutschunterricht*, 8 (1956), Heft 1, 28–45. [Also in Eichhoff and Rauch, *Der Heliand*.]

———. "Leid und Sünde im Heliand und in Otfrids Evangelienbuch." *Beiträge zur Geschichte der deutschen Sprache und Literatur*, 79 (1957), 336–79.

Russell, Jeffrey B. "St. Boniface and the Eccentrics." *Church History*, 33 (1964), 235–47.

Schmidt, Kurt Dietrich. *Die Bekehrung der Germanen zum Christentum*. Göttingen: Vandenhoeck und Ruprecht, 1939.

Schröder, Werner. *Kleinere Schriften zur althochdeutschen Sprache und Literatur*. Bern; Munich: Francke Verlag, 1966.

Scott, Mariana. *The Heliand, Translated from the Old Saxon*. Chapel Hill: University of North Carolina Press, 1966.

Sehrt, Edward Henry. *Vollständiges Wörterbuch zum Heliand und zur altsächsischen Genesis*. 2 durchgesehene Auflage. Göttingen: Vandenhoeck und Ruprecht, 1966.

Simon, Werner. *Zur Sprachmischung im Heliand*. Berlin: E. Schmidt, 1965.

Stappel, Wilhelm. *Der Heliand*. Munich: Langen-Müller, 1953.

Taeger, Burkhard. *Zahlensymbolik bei Hraban, bei Hincmar und im Heliand? Studien zur Zahlensymbolik im Frühmittelalter*. Munich: Beck, 1970.

Tietjen, Mary C. Wilson. "God, Fate, and the Hero of Beowulf." *Journal of English and German Philology* 74 (1975), 159–71.

Venerabilis Bedae Opera Historica. Ed. Carolus Plummer. Oxford: Clarendon Press, 1961.

Vilmar, A.F.C. *Deutsche Altertümer im Heliand als Einkleidung der evangelischen Geschichte*. Marburg: N.G. Elwert'sche Universitäts-Buchhandlung, 1862.

Waitz, G. *Scriptores Rerum Germanicarum, Ex Monumentis Germaniae Historicis*, vol. 7. Hannover: Hahn, 1883.

Walshe, M. O'C. *Medieval German Literature; A Survey*. London: Routledge and Kegan Paul, 1962.

Weber, Gerd Wolfgang. *Wyrd: Studien zum Schicksalsbegriff der altenglischen und altnordischen Literatur*. Bad Homburg v.d.H., Berlin; Zürich: Verlag Gehlen, 1969.

Weisweiler, Joseph, and Werner Betz. "Deutsche Frühzeit" in Friedrich Maurer and Heinz Rupp, *Deutsche Wortgeschichte*, 3. Auflage, Bd. 1. Berlin: Walter de Gruyter, 1924.

Weringha, Juw fon. *Heliand und Diatessaron*. Assen: van Gorcum, 1965.

Wicke, Hermann. *Das wunderbare Tun des heiligen Krist nach der altsächsischen Evangelienharmonie; eine Einführung in das Verständnis des "Heliand."* Göttingen: Vandenhoeck and Ruprecht, 1935.

Wiedemann, Heinrich. *Die Sachsenbekehrung*. Münster i.W.: Verlag Missionshaus Hiltrup, 1932.

Willibald. *The Life of St. Boniface.* Trans. G. W. Robinson. Cambridge: Harvard University Press, 1916.

Winston, Richard. *Charlemagne, From the Hammer to the Cross.* New York: Random House, 1954.

Wirsig, O. "Iroschotten und Bonifazius." *Deutschland*, 63 (1932). [I have been unable to locate this article. Behaghel notes it in his bibliography on p. xxxii of his eighth edition of the *Heliand* and gives the following interesting summary of its position: 'möchte im Heliand iroschottische Glaubensart finden.']

Wolf, Alois. "Beobachtungen zur ersten Fitte des Heliand." *Niederdeutsches Jahrbuch* 98/99 (1975/1976), 7–21.

Wolff, Ludwig. "Germanisches Frühchristentum im Heliand." *Zeitschrift für Deutschkunde*, 49 (1935), 37–54.

———. "Schicksal im Heliand." *Niederdeutsches Jahrbuch*, 98/99 (1975/1976), 193–96.

DATE DUE

UPI PRINTED IN U.S.A.